LEARNING THE LANGUAGE OF PRAYER

Learning the Language of Prayer

JOYCE HUGGETT

The Bible Reading Fellowship

For Lynne, with love

Text copyright © Joyce Huggett 1994

Published by
The Bible Reading Fellowship
Peter's Way, Sandy Lane West
Oxford OX4 5HG
ISBN 0 7459 2974 5
Albatross Books Pty Ltd
PO Box 320, Sutherland
NSW 2232, Australia
ISBN 0 7324 0911 X

First edition 1994
A catalogue record for this book is available
from the British Library

Printed and bound in Singapore

Acknowledgments

Scripture quotations taken from:
Good News Bible © American Bible Society
1966, 1971 and 1976. Published by The
Bible Societies and HarperCollins
The Holy Bible, New International Version
© 1973, 1978, 1984 by International Bible
Society. Used by permission of Hodder and
Stoughton Limited
The Jerusalem Bible © 1966, 1967 and
1968 by Darton, Longman & Todd and
Doubleday & Company, Inc.
The Message © 1993 by Eugene H.
Peterson. Published by NavPress, Colorado
The Holy Bible, Living Bible Edition, ©
Tyndale House Publishers 1971
The Revised Standard Version of the Bible,
© 1946, 1952, 1971 by the Division of
Christian Education of the National Council
of the Churches of Christ in the USA

Illustrations by Sister Theresa Margaret, CHN

Photographs by Quidenham Cards,
Quidenham

More information about the full range of
Quidenham Cards may be obtained by
writing to Quidenham Cards, Carmelite
Monastery, Quidenham, Norfolk,
NR16 2PH

Contents

INTRODUCTION: LEARNING THE LANGUAGE OF PRAYER

When I was six years old I found myself plunged into the world of children who could not communicate freely because they had been born with a profound hearing loss. Even at that early age, I empathized with the frustration and loneliness such children experience. A group of little deaf girls became my friends. I would play with them in the Brownie pack and in the residential school for the deaf near my home and, as far as I was able, I would attempt to understand what they were trying to say as well as painstakingly to teach them to pronounce new words—just one at a time.

These friendships gave birth to an ambition—to become a teacher of the deaf. Twenty years later that dream was realized and I spent many happy, fulfilled years watching my deaf pupils blossom as they learned to communicate: with their parents, with each other and with hearing people. Working with them underlined for me the truth of some claims once made by John Powell:

Communication is the lifeblood and heartbeat of every relationship.

If we are to enjoy deep and permanent relationships, 'effective communication is absolutely necessary'.

The suffering of noncommunication in relationships is a very real suffering... The result is loneliness, the scourge of the human spirit.[1]

Just as, deep within every deaf child, lies the longing for this lifeblood and heartbeat of relationships—to make themselves

understood and to enter into dialogue with others—so within every Christian lies the yearning to communicate with God. That is one reason why so many books have been written about prayer.

This book takes us back to basics. I make no apologies for starting at the very beginning. People beginning to learn the language of prayer can benefit from a simple manual. It gives them confidence to explore the heart of true prayer. Similarly, those who have been praying for years can benefit from a refresher course. There is always more to learn. The suggestions in this manual come, not as a book to be read at one sitting, but rather in bite-sized pieces as material to be prayed.

It is my prayer that, just as I watched the world of language liberate my deaf pupils, so learning the language of prayer will set my readers free to enjoy that great gift of God— an ever-deepening relationship with himself. This is the essence of true prayer.

1. John Powell, *Will The Real Me Please Stand Up?*

HOW TO USE THIS BOOK

Like most Bible reading notes, the material presented in this book comes in sections. On most pages there is a short Bible passage followed by a comment. These are followed either by suggestions to help readers to reflect or by a prayer to be echoed. Readers will receive most if they carve out quality time to ponder the Bible passage, assimilate the implications of the comment, embark on the project and engage in the prayer suggestions.

I also recommend that, while working their way through this book, readers keep a prayer journal. By this I mean that, having worked at the material in the way I have suggested, we write a note or a letter or a prayer to God. We then pause and write down what we believe he is saying to us in response. This is what the Psalmist appears to have done: so most of the Book of Psalms reads like a personal prayer journal. The prophets appear to have done something similar. In fact, we find God commanding Habakkuk to record the result of his prayer:

I will climb my watch-tower and wait to see what the Lord will tell me to say and what answer he will give to my complaint. The Lord gave me this answer: 'Write down clearly on clay tablets what I reveal to you, so that it can be read at a glance. Put it in writing, because it is not yet time for it to come true. But the time is coming quickly, and what I show you will come true. It may seem slow in coming, but wait for it; it will certainly take place, and it will not be delayed.'

HABAKKUK 2:1–3 (GNB)

Some benefits of journalling

Here God highlights some of the benefits of journalling. One is that when he makes a promise or gives us a revelation of some kind those words might mean little to us at the time they are spoken. Some weeks or even years later, however, they might make perfect sense. If we write them down we can refer to them when the time seems ripe. Then they will remind us of the faithfulness of God, rekindle hope and fill us with quiet joy. Another reason for journalling is that it helps to clarify what we sense we see and hear. Perhaps this was why, when John, the author of the Book of Revelation, was given a vision of Christ, he also heard God say: 'Write down what you see . . .' (Revelation 1:11, GNB).

Our journals will not be for publication but rather for private use. They will be our way of processing the lessons we are learning as we explore the language of prayer. Some people may find themselves writing poetry. Others may find themselves making their response with coloured pastels or paints or responding with a drawing.

Practicalities

Some people like to record their prayer in an attractive, hardback notebook. Others, however, find such notebooks inflexible and prefer to use a looseleaf file into which they can insert drawings, paintings, newspaper cuttings, postcards and so on. There is no right or wrong. Each person should feel free to choose for themselves.

But it can be helpful to number the pages and to keep an index so that when we want to look up at a later date what God has said to us about a certain subject, it will be easy to do so. For the same reason it can be helpful to date each entry. Because a journal is a personal, private conversation between the one who prays and God, many people worry about confidentiality. Supposing someone should read what I have written? To alleviate such anxieties, some people write 'Confidential' on the front. Some people even add a rider: 'Please destroy without reading after my death.' Others use a code which only they can understand.

The important thing to remember, as I shall repeat again at the end of this book, is to pray as you can and not as you can't. In other words, journal in a way which is helpful to you, not in a way dictated by others. Be creative. Let it assist you in learning the wonderful language of prayer.

THE ABC OF PRAYER

Nine months before writing this book I moved from England to the island of Cyprus where I now live. Very early on I set myself the task of learning Greek. Aware of this resolve, someone gave me a book and cassette to help me to learn quickly. Nine months later, I still query many of the book's claims. Like this one: 'Greek is much easier than it appears at first sight. With a little effort you will learn to cope with the 24 letters of the alphabet.'

Because I have not given language study the dedication it deserves, I still sometimes struggle to decipher the words written in Greek characters—even basic words like:

γαλα—milk

κιπos—garden

πινω—I drink

Just as, when we attempt to learn a new language, we need to commit ourselves to the hard work of mastering the alphabet with its challenge to pronounce sounds correctly, so, when we attempt to learn the language of prayer, we need to be conversant with the equivalent of its ABC. This, then, is where we begin.

Pray in secret

'Lord, teach us to pray.'
LUKE 11:1 (GNB)

In response to that request of his disciples, Jesus stressed that one of the first things we need to do as we learn the ABC of prayer is to find a prayer place:

'When you pray, go into your room, close the door, and pray.'
MATTHEW 6:6 (GNB)

I find it fascinating to discover the way today's followers of Jesus have used their creativity to rise to this challenge. An elderly lady once showed me the chair in the corner of her bedroom which was her prayer sanctuary. Although her husband was not a believer, he knew that when his wife was sitting in that chair, she was praying and was not to be disturbed.

'I go early to the office and pray before my colleagues arrive,' explained a Singaporean friend of mine who could find no place to pray in her crowded home.

And, most moving of all, was the testimony of a young wife whose unemployed husband could not tolerate the thought of his wife praying. 'So I pray in front of the television when the commercials are on—that doesn't upset my husband because my eyes are closed and he thinks I'm sleeping'!

If you have already established a prayer corner or a prayer room, or if you have ever visited a building which is

A project
Find a place where you can be alone with God. Go there regularly and ask God to help you to develop your relationship with him there.

A PRAYER

Lord God, create in me such a homesickness for you that I am compelled to find a place where I can contemplate you and meet with you.

reserved for quiet prayer, you will understand why Jesus insisted that those who are serious about learning to pray should create a prayer place. Places which are earmarked for prayer seem to be saturated with a sense of the presence of God. This powerful, prayerful atmosphere accumulates over the years and the more you visit such a place, the more you are drawn into the grand silence of God which seems to permeate every nook and cranny of the building or hover over the trees and glades and meadows or beach. Such places give rise to a heightened sense of expectancy, helping you to believe that you will encounter the God who seems to have taken up residence here in a very special way. In such places, you become acutely aware that God is there, greeting you, listening to you, blessing, restoring, nourishing and refreshing you.

Teach me
your way,
O LORD.

Ps. 27.11

Pray everywhere

A project

Today, whatever you are doing, try to be aware that God is with you, think about him and talk to him at odd moments of the day.

In the previous section we reflected on Jesus' suggestion that when we pray we should go into our room and close the door. Yet Jesus was homeless. He had nowhere to lay his head and no private place for prayer. Even so, he found a variety of hideaways where he could be alone with his Father. The Garden of Gethsemane was one. That is why Judas knew where to take those who came to arrest Jesus when he made the decision to betray him.

The hills and meadows were also places to which Jesus used to retreat. After he had fed the five thousand we read that he dismissed the crowd and after that:

. . . he went up into the hills by himself to pray. When evening came, he was there alone.

MATTHEW 14:22–23 (JB)

On another occasion:

[Jesus] went out into the hills to pray; and he spent the whole night in prayer to God.

LUKE 6:12 (JB)

It would appear that Jesus could commune with his Father anywhere and everywhere. His prayer place was portable because he encountered his Father in his heart—the Bible's word for the innermost recesses of our being.

This is the place where all real relationships are deepened. As we walk or work, we find ourselves thinking about, or even talking to, absent loved-ones—planning what we will say to them when we next meet or write or speak on the telephone. In the same way, we can cultivate an inner sanctuary which enables us to enjoy intimacy with God anywhere, any time.

Angela Ashwin, in her helpful book *Patterns not Padlocks*, suggests to young mums that they learn to sit down in the middle of chaos, if necessary, and make that a place of prayer. This is sound advice indeed. Angela is not advocating that we abandon our quiet prayer places. Far from it. She would be the first to agree that ideally most of us need to meet with God in a still place before we learn to communicate with him on the way to work, at work, at the kitchen sink, in the supermarket queue—wherever we find ourselves.

*Even when I am denied
a space to be quiet with
you,
there is still a space
inside me, Lord,
an inner room where
you are waiting for me,
and which I can enter at
any moment.*

Angela Ashwin, *Patterns not
Padlocks*, Eagle

An expectation

A project

Ask yourself: Do I believe God wants me, his child, to be happy?

Jesus not only underlines the importance of finding a place to pray, he also encourages us to expect that God will act on our behalf. His heavenly Father works for us unceasingly (see John 5:17). He is also committed to feed and clothe us:

'Look at the birds of the air; they do not sow or reap or store away in barns, and yet your heavenly Father feeds them. Are you not much more valuable than they? . . . And why do you worry about clothes? See how the lilies of the field grow. They do not labour or spin. Yet I tell you that not even Solomon in all his splendour was dressed like one of these. If that is how God clothes the grass of the field . . . will he not much more clothe you?'

MATTHEW 6:26–30 (NIV)

Using memorable picture language Jesus insists that our heavenly Father cannot give anything but good gifts to his children:

'Which of you, if his son asks for bread, will give him a stone? Or if he asks for a fish, will give him a snake? If you, then, though you are evil, know how to give good gifts to your children, how much more will your Father in heaven give good gifts to those who ask him!'

MATTHEW 7:9–11 (NIV)

This verse took on a fresh meaning for me when I moved to Cyprus. When summer comes, we occasionally see a snake sliding over the patio in our garden or hear the rustle of the grass as one slithers through a field. No Cypriot father worthy of the name would place into his child's outstretched hand a coiled, sleeping snake if that child asked for a fish. If any father did stoop to such foolishness and cruelty there would be a public outcry. Yet some Christians seem to act as though they believe God to be less loving than human fathers. If they want something very much, they assume this could not possibly be God's will. Worse, they fall into the trap of believing that the opposite must be what God wants for them. They act as though they believe that God really wants them to be miserable.

Do not look forward to what might happen tomorrow: the same everlasting Father who cares for you today will take care of you tomorrow and every day.

Francis de Sales

Pray with your eyes open

'Look at that bush!' I said to my husband as we walked to the beach one day. The bush was a mass of flame-red flowers. Framed by the cloudless blue sky, the hibiscus had filled me with awe and wonder. And it reminded me of the verse we looked at in the previous section when Jesus exclaimed: 'See how the lilies of the field grow... not even Solomon in all his splendour was dressed like one of these' (Matthew 6:28–29).

Later, I watched a small boy paddle in the sea, fill his bucket with water and shingle and, with a smile of pure delight stretching from one ear to the other, bring these treasures back to his elderly grandmother. As he fingered the water and contemplated the multi-coloured stones he had captured, her wrinkled face lit up too. These two were relishing 'the now', attentive to what they could see and feel.

Jesus' invitation to learn the ABC of prayer by looking at the lilies or by looking at the birds encourages us to do the same. Looking not only prepares us for stillness, it is important in itself.

Some people call this mindfulness. As Brother Ramon puts it in *Heaven on Earth*, mindfulness means 'to enter into, to enjoy, to absorb what is immediately before you...' He adds that to chop an onion, peel a turnip, grate a carrot and scrub a potato, if done in mindfulness, 'can be an act of meditation and a source of tranquillity and thankfulness'.

The secret of this kind of prayer is to be as alert to our surroundings as that little boy on the beach, to drink in the beauty before us, to pay attention to the sounds we so often

A project

Be still. Become attentive to the sounds around you. Ask God to make you equally attentive to his still, small voice. And today, pay attention to the smell, shape and texture of the things that you handle. Take time to gaze at the world—thanking God for the wonder of his creation.

ignore and to make it possible for all our senses to become aids to prayer: touch, smell, imagination and emotions.

A PRAYER

For the beauty of the earth,
for the beauty of the skies,
For the love which from our birth
over and around us lies,
Lord of all, to thee we raise,
This our sacrifice of praise.

Folliott Sandford Pierpoint (1835–1917)

Be real

Come as you are, that's how I love you,
Come as you are, feel quite at home,
Nothing can change the love that I bear you
All will be well, just come as you are.

That is the first verse of a song I love: it reminds me that Jesus seems to assume that we know there is only one way we can possibly come to God—and that is just as we are. Children come to accepting parents like this.

A family came to tea with me recently. The father had been away on a conference for a few days while the three children and their mother had been staying, first with the paternal grandparents and then with friends. When they all met up in my home, the baby gurgled with obvious delight as he nestled in his father's arms while from the older children tumbled story after story as they told their father about the fun they had had with his parents, the video they had seen at their friends' home and the walk they had had that morning—in the street where the little girl had been born.

Eventually excitement turned to complaint: they were bored, they were hungry, they were hot. When were we going to have tea? Could they go out to the garden to play?

In the same way as children come to loving parents just as they are, so, when Jesus prayed, he came to the Father stripped of all pretence, hiding nothing. We see this most starkly in the Garden of Gethsemane where 'grief and anguish' swept over him and he confessed: 'The sorrow in my heart is

A project
Jot down a few words or sentences which pinpoint the way you are feeling at the moment. Give those feelings to God and thank him that he accepts you just as you are.

so great that it almost crushes me . . .' Throwing himself face downwards his anguish intensified as he prayed: 'My Father, if it is possible, take this cup of suffering from me!' (Matthew 26:38–39, GNB).

Here we see Jesus being real. He refused to keep a proverbial 'stiff upper lip'. He became transparent, letting the full extent of his anguish and emotional suffering be known. If we follow his example we will come to the Father like that—just as we are.

A prayer

Just as I am . . . I come.

Cooperate with God

A project

*Think of occasions
when God has
prompted you to
partner him in helping
someone in need. Or
think of occasions
when someone has
been praying for you
and has heard God
inviting them to draw
alongside you in some
way.*

*'In prayer there is a connection between what God does and what
you do. You can't get forgiveness from God, for instance, without
also forgiving others. If you refuse to do your part, you cut yourself
off from God's part.'*

That is how Eugene Peterson paraphrases Matthew 6:14–15.
In the Good News Bible this reads:

*'If you forgive others the wrongs they have done to you, your
Father in heaven will also forgive you. But if you do not forgive
others, then your Father will not forgive the wrongs you have
done.'*

The principle is an important one which occurs over and over
again in Jesus' teaching—like the occasion in the Gospels
when the disciples warned Jesus that the crowd which had
come to hear him preach and to receive his healing touch
were very hungry. 'Send the crowd away so they can go to the
surrounding villages and countryside and find food and
lodging,' they advised Jesus. Whereupon Jesus replied: '*You*
give them something to eat' (Luke 9:12–13, NIV, emphasis
mine). They did. First they found the little food there was: five
small loaves and two tiny fish. Then they handed this to Jesus
who blessed it, placed it back into their hands and told *them* to
give it to the hungry hordes. While the disciples were obeying,
the miracle happened—the curious multiplication of the
loaves and fish meant that there was enough food for
thousands of men, women and children.

Just as Jesus gave his disciples the privilege of partnering him as he performed this particular miracle, so he often invites us to cooperate with him in becoming, at least in part, the answer to our own prayers. That is why it is important, not simply to tell God that someone is in need and to ask him to alleviate that need, but also to wait and to listen just in case he asks us to visit the person concerned or to telephone or to write or to help in some other way.

A PRAYER

O God, you claim me as
your partner,
respecting me,
trusting me,
tussling with me.
Support me
as I dare to be
vulnerable with you,
encourage me
as I dare take risks with
you,
so together we can
transform our world.

Bridget Rees, quoted in Janet
Morley, *Bread of Tomorrow,*
Christian Aid and SPCK, 1992

Practise fasting

A project

Reflect on this claim:

'Perhaps in our affluent society fasting involves far larger sacrifice than the giving of money'

(Richard Foster, *Celebration of Discipline*, Hodder and Stoughton, page 47).

As we have reflected on the alphabet of prayer, we have been caught up in a number of paradoxes. We have observed that, like Jesus, we can pray anywhere and everywhere; yet there is special value in having a prayer place. We have also seen that we can pray at any time; but there is value in making and keeping appointments with God. And we have highlighted the importance of coming to God with great expectations: that he will hear, bless and reward us; that, equally, we need to come with all our antennae out, ready to receive what he longs to give.

Before we move on to consider another stage of learning the language of prayer, we need to reflect on one more assumption Jesus appears to make—that our praying will be accompanied by fasting.

'And now about fasting. When you fast, giving up your food for a spiritual purpose, don't do it publicly, as the hypocrites do, who try to look wan and dishevelled so people will feel sorry for them. Truly, that is the only reward they will ever get. But when you fast, look your best, so that no one will suspect you are hungry, except your Father who knows every secret. And he will reward you.'
MATTHEW 6:16–18 (LB)

Jesus not only said, 'When you pray . . .' Almost in the same breath, he continues, 'When you fast . . .' He did not say, 'If you fast . . .' but, 'When you fast . . .' It was as though, in his mind, fasting and prayer are two sides of the same coin. Furthermore, when John's disciples asked why his disciples did not fast, Jesus replied:

'How can the guests of the bridegroom mourn while he is with them? The time will come when the bridegroom will be taken from them; then they will fast.'

MATTHEW 9:15 (NIV)

One reason why fasting is valuable is that it helps to expose the things that control us. Food so easily camouflages and quietens emotions which consume us: anger, impatience, anxiety, loneliness, self-loathing. If we decide to deprive the body of one meal a week or of all meals one day a week, these obsessional feelings will rise to the surface. Although this can be distressing, it reveals some of the hindrances to our prayer life we need to deal with. But fasting has a positive face too. It sharpens our concentration so that we can use the time we would have spent preparing or eating food praising God and deepening our relationship with him.

Pray that you may take seriously Jesus' invitation to find a time and a place to pray, a rhythm of prayer which works for you for now and that your praying and worshipping will be laced by fasting.

LEARNING SOME BASIC VOCABULARY

The reason I wanted to learn Greek was that I longed to be able to communicate with my neighbours—particularly with those who speak little or no English. But in addition to struggling with the alphabet, so that I could read and write the language, I realized that I would not achieve my main aim until I became familiar with the basic words the locals used. So I learned everyday words like 'good morning', 'hello', 'good evening', 'good night', 'please', 'yes' and so on.

When we start to learn the vocabulary of prayer, we discover that there are certain words which people frequently use about prayer. In this section of the book, we seek to understand what these words mean so that we can also use them freely and intelligently.

Intercession

One of the words people use frequently about prayer is 'intercession'. In fact, if you listen to some people talk about prayer, you might fall into the trap of believing that prayer and intercession are synonymous. This is understandable since intercession is a vital facet of prayer and since Jesus clearly expects us to intercede for others.

To intercede means being a bridge on which God and a particular person, a group of people or a certain situation meet. In other words, it means burden-bearing on behalf of others. Just as four men carried their paralysed friend to Jesus in the hope that Jesus would heal him, so we carry people and situations to God trusting that he will intervene on their behalf. Intercession is therefore a costly, selfless way of loving people and the world.

Jesus exhorts us to intercede. Take Luke chapter 10, for example:

'The harvest is plentiful, but the workers are few. Ask the Lord of the harvest, therefore, to send out workers into his harvest field.'
LUKE 10:2 (NIV)

In a cluster of parables, he encourages us to 'ask' (Luke 11:5–8) and to go on and on asking with earnestness, perseverance, humility and intensity (see Luke 18:1–8, 10–14; Mark 13:33; 14:38; 11:24 for example).

When we take seriously his challenge to pray with humility, the nature of our intercessory prayer may well change. Some people spend a great deal of time describing a

problem or a crisis to God as though he, the all-seeing One, knows nothing of the situation about which we feel so deeply. They then proceed to tell him how to solve the problem as though they have forgotten that he is all-wise as well as all-powerful. In his graciousness and generosity, God hears these prayers but he gently calls us into a more costly, more authentic way of interceding. He shows us that he, himself, is the eternal intercessor: 'He . . . is at the right hand of God . . . and is also interceding for us' (Romans 8:34, NIV).

He convinces us that, since he started praying for the people or situation long before we did and since he is far wiser than we are, our responsibility is to seek to discover the nature of his prayer and to echo it rather than to counteract his prayer with our own requests. He shows us that this inevitably means listening and waiting rather than clamouring and dictating—that we need him to interpret the feebleness of our prayer. When we echo the prayer of Jesus, we find that we pray, not from our lips only, but from our hearts. In fact we may quickly come to the place where we run out of words and we weep or groan or, more conscious of God's greatness than the enormity of the problem, we simply hold a person or a crisis into his love.

A project

33

In many parts of the world there is a need for skilled professional people: doctors, nurses, teachers, engineers, physiotherapists, secretaries and others. Do what Jesus begs. Pray that more people will respond to his call to leave the comfort-zone of home and go to those who need them.

How to intercede

A project

Ponder this claim:

'We must be willing to have our peace disturbed. To pray in silence with a newspaper headline before our eyes will pull us from the silence of self-contemplation into the intercession of Christ'

(David Runcorn, *Space for God*, DLT, 1990, pages 128–29).

In the previous section we examined the much-used word 'intercession' and homed in on Jesus' expectation that we will pray persistently and patiently: 'Watch and pray . . .' (Matthew 26:41, NIV). 'Ask and it will be given to you; seek and you will find; knock and the door will be opened to you . . .' (Luke 11:9, NIV).

Today, we concentrate on some ways of interceding. The first thing to remember is that we do not have huge problems and a miniscule God. We have a great God and life-sized problems. When we intercede we need to remind ourselves of the omnipotence and omnipresence of God. This helps us to do what Jesus asks, to pray in faith.

Next, we need to recognize that we are not called to pray for everything and everyone. God gives us a burden when he wants us to pray. This burden will not always be felt when we are on our knees in prayer. Very often it will come at unexpected times during the day—when a colleague or a friend is in need, when we watch the news or read the newspaper, when we encounter the homeless or destitute. So we need to be prepared to intercede while we work or walk, while we clean the car or do the shopping.

Take watching the news, for example. It sometimes happens that, as we watch the screen, a particular person or situation will make an impact on us. There and then, while our eyes are fixed on the screen, we can be aware of God's love and simply hold the person or the crisis into that love. Or, while reading the newspaper, a similar sensation might sweep over us. This should not be ignored but rather should be translated into prayer. We might find ourselves so drawn into the feelings of the person or their relatives or the immensity of the need of the situation that we find ourselves hurting off and on during the day. This pain and concern can be translated into a brief prayer like, 'Lord, have mercy,' or we can rest assured that as we groan inwardly, God is interpreting those sighs and groans and joining them with the prayer Jesus is making for these same people or situations.

Another way in which God might prompt us to pray is to alert us to problems which we have been contending with recently. Maybe we have been through a period of depression or we are in danger of losing our job; perhaps our marriage is going through turbulent times or we are feeling lonely. When we are in touch with our own pain, we can use it prayerfully to hold into the love of God people all over the world who are suffering similarly. It does not necessarily change our own situation but it redeems and uses it.

Ask God to teach you to speak the language of intercession.

Meditation

Like 'intercession', 'meditation' is another word which people often use about prayer. But Christian meditation must not be confused with yoga, Eastern meditation or transcendental meditation. For, unlike these disciplines, Christian meditation has nothing to do with emptying our minds. Christian meditation engages every part of us—our mind, our emotions, our imagination, our creativity and, supremely, our will.

As Archbishop Anthony Bloom puts it, 'Meditation is a piece of straight thinking under God's guidance.' Yet it is not the same as an academic study of the Scriptures. This becomes clear when we listen to the Psalmist describing his practice of meditation:

On my bed I think of you,
I meditate on you all night long...
PSALM 63:6 (JB)

The word for 'meditate' which is used here means to 'mutter' or to 'murmur persistently', repeating the same words over and over again. In Psalm 119, the Psalmist uses a different word when he refers to meditation:

I mean to meditate on your precepts
and to concentrate on your paths.
PSALM 119:15 (JB)

Though princes put me on trial,
your servant will meditate on your statutes.
PSALM 119:23 (JB)

37

A project

In Psalm 77, the Psalmist promises God:

I will meditate on all your works
and consider all your mighty deeds.
PSALM 77:12 (NIV)

Look back on your own life and the things you have read and heard about God. Record and remind yourself over and over again of his greatness and his faithfulness. In this way, you will be meditating like the Psalmist.

A PRAYER

*May my meditation be
pleasing to him,
as I rejoice in the Lord.*

Psalm 104:34 (NIV)

*I stretch out my hands to your beloved commandments,
I meditate on your statutes.*

PSALM 119:48 (JB)

The word he uses in these verses means 'to muse', 'to ponder', 'to reflect', 'to consider'. In other words, Christian meditation involves, not emptiness, but fullness. It means being attentive to God. The purpose of this attentiveness, this reflecting and this pondering is, among other things, to see ourselves in the light of God's revealed word—just as Jesus weighed each of Satan's subtle temptations against the teaching of the Old Testament. We meditate to give God's words the opportunity to penetrate, not just our minds, but our emotions—the places where we hurt—and our will—the place where we make choices and decisions. We meditate to encounter the Living Word, Jesus himself. We meditate so that every part of our being, our thoughts and our affections and our ambitions, are turned to face and honour and glorify him. Yet another reason for learning to meditate is so that we may become conversant with the will of God.

With this last aim in mind, Richard Foster claims that 'meditation is the necessary prelude to intercession'.[1] As we saw in 'Intercession', when we intercede we need to discern how Jesus is praying in any given situation. So we need to learn to listen, to wait, to interpret. This comes, not through academic study alone, but through meeting with the living Lord and meditating on his words.

1. Richard Foster, *Celebration of Discipline*, Hodder and Stoughton

How to meditate

A project

Ponder this claim:

Meditation is a God-ordained channel by which truth from God, written in the Scriptures, enters our minds, passes into our hearts and causes us to adore and love God and desire to serve him more.

Peter Toon, *Meditating Upon God's Word*, DLT, 1988, page 34

We have seen that the English word 'meditation' may be variously translated by words like muttering and murmuring, reflecting and recollecting, musing and pondering. With these hidden meanings in mind, it becomes apparent that Jesus meditated on the Scriptures. He knew the Old Testament so well that he easily made the connection between biblical truth and what was happening to him at various stages of his life. In Luke 4, three times Satan tries to deflect him from doing God's work in God's way; three times he combats Satan's suggestions by quoting Scripture:

The devil led him up to a high place and showed him in an instant all the kingdoms of the world. And he said to him, 'I will give you all their authority and splendour, for it has been given to me, and I can give it to anyone I want to. So if you worship me, it will all be yours.'

Jesus answered, 'It is written: "Worship the Lord your God and serve him only."'

LUKE 4:5–8 (NIV)

Here Jesus is revealing that Deuteronomy 6:13 has become so much a part of his thinking and behaving that it automatically springs to mind and affects his attitude when faced with Satan's subtle ploys.

Scripture can similarly become a part of our make-up if we meditate on it. And the best way to prepare to meditate is to respond to the invitation God gives us through the Psalmist: 'Be still, and know that I am God' (Psalm 46:10).

In the stillness we can shed some of the pressures which would prevent us receiving God's Word into the innermost core of our being. We can focus away from the mundane and the everyday and onto God. Such stillness is to Bible reading what preparing the soil is to good farming. Essential for fruitfulness.

When we have become still, if we read a passage of Scripture which we have previously studied or some verses which refer to something which is troubling us, we may well find that a verse or a phrase or a sentence or a pen picture will draw us to itself. If it does, there is no need to read on. Instead, we should stop to reflect and to treasure the words, to turn them over and over in our minds, repeating them until the truth which they contain trickles from our head into our hearts.

All our faculties can be enlisted to help us meditate. The mind enables us to understand what the words mean as we read them in context. The memory helps us recall what we have learned and experienced of God's character and faithfulness in the past. The imagination is a God-given gift which the prophets used to picture the insights God entrusted them with and which Jesus used to describe his kingdom. (So he likens his Father to a faithful shepherd, a Middle Eastern housewife and a loving, Middle Eastern father, Luke 15.) And the emotions enable us to identify with the characters in the passage we are reading.

A PRAYER

May the words of my mouth and the meditation of my heart be pleasing in your sight,
O Lord, my Rock and my Redeemer.

Psalm 19:14 (NIV)

Contemplation

'Meditation' and 'contemplation' are often used interchangeably. This is understandable because certain similarities suggest that the two forms of prayer are synonymous. Like meditation, contemplation involves putting ourselves into the hands of God so that he can change and transform our attitudes, perceptions and behaviour. Like meditation, contemplation involves listening intently to the Word of God. And like meditation, contemplation requires stillness in order that we may open ourselves to God and his penetrating, powerful Word.

But meditation and contemplation are also marked by certain differences so they should not be confused with each other. Thomas Merton summed it up when he said: 'Contemplation is nothing else but the perfection of love.' Or, as others have defined it, contemplation is the prayer of loving regard, the prayer of loving attentiveness, the art of paying rapt and loving attention to God and his world.

Contemplation is about growing in love. If we take the work of contemplation seriously, we cannot escape the theme of love—of God's inexhaustible love for us, for people everywhere, for the whole creation . . . Contemplation is to know and love God perfectly in the depths of your being.[1]

Contemplation goes further and deeper than meditation. While the person meditating mutters and muses on God's word, the contemplative pays silent attention to Jesus, the living Word— the one who is central to their prayer. Indeed, contemplation goes one step further. Contemplation goes beyond words and symbols and concepts to the reality words and concepts describe. As Jim Borst describes it, 'In praying the words, "our Father in heaven", for example, we go beyond the words to an awareness of God's presence deep within us and dwell in that presence. The actual words become rather like the ringing of a bell awakening us from sleep to a consciousness of Christ's indwelling presence.'[2] When we are drawn by God's Spirit into this kind of reality, although our minds may not be able to explain the nature of our encounter with God, by love we *can* discern what is happening. This love may cause us to cry out:

You yourself are my contemplation
You are my delight
You for your own sake
I seek above me.
From you yourself
I feed within me.
You are the field
In which I labour.
You are the food
For which I labour.
You are my cause
You are my effect
You are my beginning
You are my end, without end.
You are for me
Eternity.

My adaptation of a twelfth-century meditation of Isaac of Stella

1. Jim Borst, *Coming to God*, Eagle, 1992

2. ibid., page 48

How to contemplate

A project

If you sense within yourself a hunger for this kind of prayer it is probably a sign that the Holy Spirit is leading you into a deeper awareness of God and his love. Try to carve out time when you can come into his presence in the way I describe. Follow this up by reading some of the books mentioned in the bibliography at the back of this book. Or talk to others who have travelled down this well-trodden path.

Contrary to much current thinking, contemplation has nothing to do with making our minds blank or having honey-sweet thoughts. As we have observed, its chief aim is to encounter Christ so that our love for him is rekindled.

If this is to happen, we need to set aside uninterrupted time for contemplative prayer. Such prayer begins, to borrow the imagery of John Donne, by 'tuning the instrument at the gate'—that is by preparing our hearts to pray even before we enter our place of prayer. We can do this while we tidy our room or drive home from work because it is an attitude of mind and heart rather than an activity.

When we enter our prayer place, we need to give ourselves time to relax in God's presence. One of the best ways of doing this is to recognize some of the reasons why we are tense: worry, pressure of things to be done, the quarrel we just had with our spouse or a colleague. It will be impossible to contemplate until these pressures have been handed over to God. When we transfer them to him, we find ourselves gloriously free with an uncluttered expanse of time in which to be met afresh by him. Perhaps that is one reason why Peter invites us to: 'Cast all your anxiety on him because he cares for you' (1 Peter 5:7).

Having transferred our burdens and having allowed the tensions to slide from us as snow slides from the roof-tops in the thaw, the next phase of prayer involves becoming aware of the presence of God. Jesus has promised that he will never leave us or forsake us. We take time to tune into his presence,

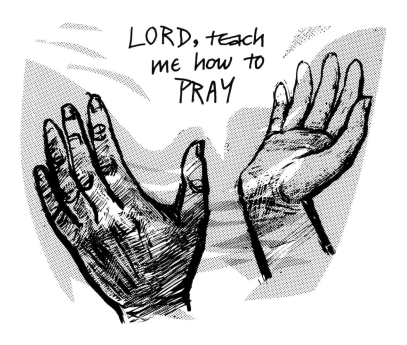

LORD, ~~teach~~ me how to PRAY

A PRAYER

*Lord, teach me how to
pray.
Glorify your name in
my life.
May your Spirit go on
and on praying in me
and through me
and for me
that your will may be
done in my life
now and always.*

aware that he is on our side—he is *for us*. As Jim Borst traces this process in his life-changing book *Coming to God*, we then spend time clearing from our path any obstacles which would prevent us from gazing on God. So we surrender every part of ourselves to him, seek to accept what is happening in our lives at this moment in time and repent of those things which would obscure our vision of God or prevent us from hearing his voice and knowing his love. We seek to receive his forgiveness and let go of any bitterness we feel against others. With these obstacles removed, we are ready for the moment of contemplation. 'Your prayer is nothing but a loving awareness of him: "I look because I love: I look in order to love, and my love is fed and influenced by looking." '[1]

In the quietness, aware of his presence, we open our hearts to receive his love. The prayer is usually wordless and fed by a deep desire for him. This leads us on to a place where instead of seeking God, we are found by him. We discover that, long before we came to our place of prayer, he was seeking us. So he responds to our longing. We bask in the warmth of his love. We feel his gaze on us. He fills us afresh with his Spirit. We receive a new perspective on life—his perspective. We draw so close to his heart that we sense his concern for the world, and from our contemplation flows intercession as we catch his compassion for a hurting world.

1. Jim Borst, *Coming to God*, Eagle, 1992

Adoration

The prayer of contemplation almost always progresses into the prayer of adoration or, to give it its other name, worship. This progression is natural. When we have felt afresh the loving touch of God, our hearts go out to him in 'wonder, love and praise'. Or, as Richard Foster has described this form of prayer:

In adoration we enter the rarefied air of selfless devotion. We ask for nothing but to cherish him. We seek nothing but his exaltation. We focus on nothing but his goodness. 'In the prayer of adoration we love God for himself, for his very being, for his radiant joy.'[1]

I recall an occasion when meditation and contemplation led very naturally and irresistibly into the adoration of the invisible but risen Christ. It was Easter Day and I was leading a retreat on the island of Cyprus. Several of the retreatants and I determined that, just as the women had gone to the tomb before daybreak on the first Easter Day, so we would go to the cave where we had held our outdoor service of worship on Good Friday. So, at 5.30 a.m., we met and walked together, in silence, to our 'tomb'. By the time we reached our destination, the first flush of light was dispelling the darkness so I read aloud those spine-tingling words from John 20:1.

Early on the first day of the week, while it was still dark, Mary Magdalene went to the tomb and saw that the stone had been removed from the entrance . . .

As the darkness disappeared, we stood at the mouth of the cave and meditated on this story. Gradually, we watched the

A project

John of the Cross once asked someone what their prayer consisted of. The person simply replied that prayer, for her, consisted of 'considering the beauty of God and in rejoicing that he has such beauty'. How might you have answered that question?

A PRAYER

Jesus, we love you
We worship and adore
you
Glorify your name in all
the earth.

sky begin to glow as though the sun was warning us that it was about to rise. As it peeped over the black mountain mass and gradually rolled, round and golden, into the cloudless sky, I gently pressed the play button of the tape player I had brought with me. The words of the aria from *The Messiah*: 'I know that my Redeemer liveth' put many of us in touch with our deep-down belief that: 'Christ has died, Christ is risen, Christ will come again.' By the time the aria had finished, the sun hung suspended in the sky—a symbol of the resurrection. All of us stood speechless—not with euphoria but with a deeper emotion: an adoration which words would have trivialized. So we continued to stand in silent praise and we walked back to breakfast in silence. We ate breakfast in silence while we continued to listen to *The Messiah*:

Worthy . . . is the Lamb that was slain
And hath redeemed us to God by his blood.
To receive power and riches and wisdom and strength
and honour and glory and blessing.

As we listened, I sensed I understood what adoration really means. And I knew from the faces and eyes and awed silence of many of the others that they were in touch with the same well-spring of speechless adoration. In the silence of our hearts we were proclaiming Jesus' 'worthship' which is what adoration and worship really mean.

1. Richard Foster, *Prayer*, Hodder and Stoughton, 1992, page 86

Confession

The closer we come to Christ through the prayer of contemplation, the more conscious we shall become of our need to confess our sins to him and to repent. 'Confession' is another of those words which people often use about prayer. In the Old Testament the word has a medley of meanings. It means an acknowledgment of sin and guilt. Yet the sense of heart-felt gratitude and praise that God is slow to anger and compassionate is also present, together with an awareness that God is a God who forgives. The Psalm David wrote after he had been convicted of committing adultery with the wife of one of his trusted employees is a perfect example of this kind of confession:

Using your God-given imagination, put yourself in the place of that small boy. How do you feel as you sense and see the heavenly Father's love? Pray out of the experience.

Have mercy on me, O God, in your goodness,
in your great tenderness wipe away my faults;
wash me clean of my guilt,
purify me from my sin.

For I am well aware of my faults,
I have my sin constantly in my mind,
having sinned against none other than you,
having done what you regard as wrong.
PSALM 51:1–4 (JB)

The emphasis in this prayer of confession is not primarily on David's guilt, though clearly he is ever conscious of his culpability. The emphasis, rather, is on the effect his self-centredness has had on the Father-heart of God.

A PRAYER

*Create in me a new,
clean heart, O God,
filled with clean
thoughts and right
desires.*

Psalm 51:10 (LB)

I once heard a story which helped me to refocus my attention away from my own innate sinfulness and to concentrate, instead, on the way sin breaks the heart of God.

The story was of a small boy who was consistently late home from school. This caused his parents great anxiety. They cautioned him and threatened him but he continued to disobey them and to arrive home late. One day his parents warned him that the next time he was late he would be given no dinner. For a few days he arrived home on time but then he resorted to his old habit, dawdling on the way home and arriving much later than the prescribed time.

When the family sat down to their evening meal—the boy's favourite: roast chicken, roast potatoes, vegetables and gravy—his mother placed a large plateful of steaming hot food in front of his father, and a plateful in her own place while, in front of her son, she put an empty plate. The boy's father said, 'Let's thank God for our food.' So they all closed their eyes while he said grace. When the boy opened his eyes, he saw his father exchanging his empty plate for his own plate full of food.

As the boy gazed at his father's empty plate, two things struck him very deeply—the depth of his father's love and the price he was prepared to pay to express that love. This melted the boy's hardness and prompted him to determine to change his ways.

Incarnation

Just as confession is a natural off-shoot of contemplative prayer so is what is sometimes called the prayer of incarnation. The word 'incarnation' comes from two Latin words 'in carne'—in the flesh. These bring us to the root of incarnational prayer.

C.S. Lewis describes incarnational prayer powerfully. Commenting on the phrase from the Lord's Prayer, 'Your will be done,' he writes:

A great deal of it is to be done by God's creatures, including me. The petition, then, is not merely that I may patiently suffer God's will but also that I may vigorously do it. I must be an agent as well as a patient. I am asking that I may be enabled to do it . . .

Taken this way, I find the words have a more regular daily application. For . . . there are always duties to be done, usually, for me, neglected duties to be caught up with. 'Thy will be done— by me—now' brings one back to brass tacks.[1]

Jesus shows us some of the ways in which we may 'flesh out' our prayer. Describing the day when he will take his place on his glorious throne with all the nations gathered at his feet, he shows how those who have lived their prayer will be rewarded. He will say to them:

'Enter, you who are blessed by my Father! Take what's coming to you in this kingdom. It's been ready for you since the world's foundation. And here's why:
I was hungry and you fed me.
I was thirsty and you gave me a drink.

A PRAYER

You asked for my hands that you might use them for your purpose.
I gave them for a moment then withdrew them for the work was hard.

You asked for my mouth to speak out against injustice.
I gave you a whisper that I might not be accused.

You asked for my eyes to see the pain of poverty.
I closed them for I did not want to see.

You asked for my life that you might work through me.
I gave a small part that I might not get too involved.

Lord, forgive my calculated efforts to serve you, only when it is convenient for me to do so, only in those places where it is safe to do so, and only with those who make it easy to do so.[2]

A project

Ask yourself, 'What prevents me from incarnating my prayer in the way Jesus and others describe?'

I was homeless and you gave me a room.
I was shivering and you gave me clothes.
I was sick and you stopped to visit.
I was in prison and you came to me.'
'Then those "sheep" are going to say, "Master, what are you talking about? When did we ever see you hungry and feed you, thirsty and give you a drink? And when did we ever see you sick or in prison and come to you?" Then the King will say, "I'm telling the solemn truth: whenever you did one of these things to someone overlooked and ignored, that was me—you did it to me." '

PARAPHRASE OF MATTHEW 25, EUGENE PETERSON, *THE MESSAGE*

These verses motivate much of the magnificent work which Mother Teresa of Calcutta does. Writing to her sisters, she says:

Hear Jesus your co-worker speak to you:
'I want you to be my fire of love amongst the poor, the sick, the dying, and the little children: the poor I want you to bring to me.' Learn this sentence by heart and when you are wanting in generosity, repeat it. We can refuse Christ just as we refuse others: 'I will not give you my hands to work with, my feet to walk with, my mind to study with, my heart to love with. You knock at the door, but I will not give you the key of my heart.' This is what he feels so bitterly: not being able to live his life in a soul.[3]

1. C.S. Lewis, *Letters to Malcolm Chiefly on Prayer*, Bles, 1964, page 40

2. Joe Seremane, 'South Africa', quoted in Janet Morley, editor, *Bread of Tomorrow*, Christian Aid, 1992, page 85

3. Mother Teresa, *Jesus, the Word to be Spoken*, Fount, 1990, page 80

Petition

A project

Try to anticipate what you will need in the next 24 hours. In your prayer journal, divide a page into two columns. At the top of the first column, write the heading Requests and at the top of the second column, write the heading Answers. In the first column, write a list of words which summarize what you sense you will need from God today. Tomorrow, or on subsequent days, return to your list to fill in the answers. Catherine Marshall advocated this prayer practice calling it a 'faith booster.'

The final word in the vocabulary of prayer which we shall look at in this book is 'petition', which means to make a request for ourselves.

Some people hesitate to use this kind of prayer fearing that it is selfish. Yet Jesus actively encourages us to ask him for even mundane things like our staple diet. In the Lord's Prayer, for example, he has us praying: 'Give us today the food we need' (Matthew 6:11, GNB).

The implication is that he loves us enough to be concerned about us when we are hungry or when we are thirsty, when we are sick or in any emotional need or when we have lost something important. He wants us to tell him about these needs in the same way as we encourage our children or our friends to share their needs with us.

But some Christians protest that such sharing is superfluous. Since God is all-knowing, he sees what we need before we tell him. What such people forget is that God *likes* us to talk to him about our concerns. He knows that, sometimes, in spreading them before him, we gain a new perspective or new energy to cope. At other times, when he grants our requests, our relationship with him will be strangely enriched and deepened simply because we were humble enough to ask.

Catherine Marshall used to call this the prayer of helplessness: 'When achievement has come because of our helplessness linked to God's power, it has a rightness about it that no amount of self-inspired striving can have.'[1] I have personally found this to be very true in my own life and am therefore grateful that God has woven the principle of need and helplessness into the very fabric of our lives: that he wants us to share with him our inadequacy so that he can share with us his inexhaustible sufficiency.

'But so often God says "no" when I ask him for something,' some Christians complain. God does sometimes refuse to give us our heart's desire but such refusals are never born from stinginess—only from love. As C.S. Lewis once observed: 'If God had granted all the silly prayers I've made in my life, where should I be now?' And as someone else has shrewdly seen the situation, one day, if not on earth, then in heaven, we shall be given the wisdom to see why God's 'no' lay in our best interests. Before that day, a major part of our petitionary prayer should be for wisdom and discernment that we may know the mind of Christ in any given situation and therefore instinctively pray the prayer he is praying for us.

Dear Father,
I don't want to treat you
like Santa Claus but I do
need to ask things of
you. Give me, please,
food to eat today. I'm
not asking for
tomorrow, but I am
asking for today ...

1. Catherine Marshall,
Beyond Ourselves

FINDING A TUTOR

A friend of mine moved to Cyprus at the same time as I did. Because he lives in a small village where few people speak English, he has worked far harder at language study than I have. Instead of relying on books and cassettes, he attends language lessons and has employed the services of a private tutor. Consequently, he is becoming confident and fluent as his grasp of this fascinating language rapidly improves.

When it comes to learning the language of prayer, we all have an individual, indwelling tutor: God's Holy Spirit. In this section of the book, we discover what he is like and how he accomplishes his tutorial work.

The Holy Spirit's role

A project

Reflect on an insight of William Temple:

It is no good giving me a play like Hamlet *or* King Lear *and telling me to write a play like that. Shakespeare could do it: I can't. And it is no good showing me a life like the life of Jesus and telling me to live a life like that. Jesus could do it; I can't. But if the genius of Shakespeare could come and live in me, then I could write plays like that. And if the Spirit of Jesus could come and live in me, I could live a life like that.*

The Holy Spirit plays a vital role in teaching us to pray. Was this one reason why, between his resurrection and his ascension, Jesus said to his disciples: 'Do not leave Jerusalem, but wait for the gift my Father promised, which you have heard me speak about . . . In a few days you will be baptised with the Holy Spirit' (Acts 1:4–5, NIV)?

We are not told precisely why Jesus told his disciples to wait. We are told who the Holy Spirit is and before we examine what our prayer tutor teaches us, we need to remind ourselves of the way Jesus describes him.

Jesus refers to him in John 14:26 as the Paraclete—a Greek word which is variously translated the Comforter, the Advocate or the Counsellor. The Paraclete means someone called to the side of another because they are qualified to help—like the doctor we call when we are sick or the solicitor we employ when we need legal advice. But Jesus not only calls the Holy Spirit the Comforter, he deliberately describes him as 'another Comforter' (John 14:16). The word used for 'another' means one 'of the same kind'. The implication is that this Comforter, the Holy Spirit, is just like Jesus: 'Jesus' other self.'

Like Jesus, then, the Holy Spirit is an attractive personality. This becomes apparent when Paul lists some of the fruit he produces in the believer: 'The Spirit produces love, joy, peace, patience, kindness, goodness, faithfulness, humility, and self-control' (Galatians 5:22, GNB).

Commenting on this spiritual harvest Robert Frost observes: 'Only a lovely person can minister love. Only a joyful person can minister joy. Only a peaceful person can minister peace.' This lovely, joyful, peaceful person empowers us, enabling us to do what we could not do alone—including discovering how to pray.

Thank God that his Spirit has come and that part of his mission is to teach us to pray while another part is to pray through us.

The Spirit convinces us we are loved

A project

On the first Easter evening, Jesus appeared to his disciples as they gathered together in the Upper Room. There John reminds us that 'he breathed on them and said, "Receive the Holy Spirit"' (John 20:22, NIV). Try to imagine that you are there in the room with the disciples and that Jesus comes to you and says those words. Allow him to breathe his breath and energy and personality into you.

Without the Holy Spirit we cannot pray. He is not simply our prayer tutor. He is far more than that. He helps us to pray like Jesus. In his letter to the Romans, Paul explains that one reason is that it is the Holy Spirit who enables us to call God 'Abba, Father'. Furthermore, 'The Spirit himself testifies with our spirit that we are God's children' (Romans 8:15–16).

Some people protest that they cannot possibly call God 'Daddy' because of the hurts which have been inflicted on them by their earthly fathers. When such people see how close Jesus was to his Father and it is suggested that, like Jesus, they come to the heavenly Father full of trust and confidence, they feel disadvantaged. But if we take Paul's teaching seriously, the past need no longer present us with an insurmountable obstacle. The Holy Spirit can either by-pass it to convince us that God is a loving parent-figure and that we are his children, or, as he so often does, he can come into our bruised and battered emotions and heal us. When this happens, the veil is removed from our eyes and we recognize that, although our earthly father may have failed us for a whole variety of reasons, our heavenly Father is not like that. His love for us is unconditional and never-ending. It always enfolds us.

This truth is liberating. Breathtaking. When it trickles from our head into our heart, it transforms our prayer life.

Spirit divine, attend our prayers,
And make this house thy home;
Descend with all thy gracious power,
O come, great Spirit, come!

Come as the wind, sweep clean away
What dead within us lies,
And search and freshen all our souls
With living energies.

The Spirit gives access to the Father

A project

Meditate on Jesus' claim: 'God is Spirit, and only by the power of his Spirit can people worship him as he really is' (John 4:24, GNB).

We have observed that the Holy Spirit is the one who sets us free to call God Father. But Paul reminds us that he does more than that. Together with Jesus, he gives us access to the heavenly Father: 'It is through Christ that all of us, Jews and Gentiles, are able to come in the one Spirit into the presence of the Father' (Ephesians 2:18, GNB).

Francis Wale Oke comments on this verse: 'God is Spirit. We cannot contact Him through our intellect, our mind or our body. We can only contact God through our spirit. It is the Spirit of God that helps our spirit to have direct contact with God.'[1]

Rublev's famous icon of the Holy Trinity, or 'The Circle of Love' as it is sometimes called, helps me to understand this. Andrei Rublev, the fifteenth-century iconographer, painted this picture to help Christians grasp this mystery and be drawn into the love which flows so freely between the Father, the Son and the Holy Spirit. The picture is made up of three angels sitting in a circle. The angel on the right represents the Holy Spirit, the angel on the left represents the heavenly Father and in the centre of the circle sits the Son. The movement of the heads makes it clear that, if the person of prayer wants to move into this circle, they must do so through the person on the right, the Holy Spirit. His head is inclined towards the Son whose head, in turn, leans towards the Father. In other words, pictorially, Andrei Rublev is saying just what Paul said so succinctly—that if we want to find the way to the Father, we come through Jesus by his Spirit. In turn, this reminds us that a rich and relevant prayer life exists only with the help and inspiration of the Holy Spirit.

Lord Christ...
Without your Holy
Spirit
who lives in our hearts,
what would we be?
You open for us a way
towards faith,
towards trust in God...
Spirit of the Risen
Christ,
Spirit of compassion,
Spirit of praise,
your love for each one
of us
will never go away.

Brother Roger of Taizé

1. Francis Wale Oke, *Alone With God*, Highland, page 104

The Holy Spirit reveals Jesus to us

A project

Respond to this challenge:

'To be filled with the Spirit . . . is not an option; it is a necessity, it is God's command: "be filled with the Spirit" (Ephesians 5:18).'

Francis Wale Oke, *Alone With God*, Highland, page 113

A PRAYER

Father, I pray that out of the wealth of your glory
You will strengthen my inner being with your Spirit,
So that Christ will make his home in my heart
And so that I may have my roots in love
and make love the foundation of my entire existence.
I pray that you will reveal to me just how broad and long
how high and deep
The love of Christ is,
So that I may be filled to overflowing with the very nature of Christ.

An adaptation of Ephesians 3:14–21

The icon I described in 'The Spirit gives access to the Father', the icon of the Holy Trinity, is best viewed through a circle—a ring formed with the index finger and the thumb or a real ring. This highlights the circle in which the three angels sit and emphasizes that, if we want to come to Jesus, we come via the Holy Spirit. Pictorially the icon is portraying a vital theological truth which Paul sums up succinctly when he prays that God would give the Christians in Ephesus 'the Spirit, who will make you wise and reveal God to you, so that you will know him' (Ephesians 1:17, GNB).

Jesus also makes it clear that, among other things, the Holy Spirit's mission is to make God known to the believer. He does this in a whole variety of ways. One is through our intellect, by reminding us of all that Jesus said and did (John 14:26), by confirming that Jesus really is who he claimed to be (John 15:26), by bringing glory to the Son (John 16:14) and by interpreting Jesus' mind and teaching (John 16:14).

Another is in the depths of our hearts by leading us into 'complete truth' (John 16:7, 13). Commenting on the phrase, 'the complete truth', Henri Nouwen explains that the word 'truth' is closely related to the word 'betrothal'. The Holy Spirit will lead us into full intimacy with God.

Since all effective prayer stems from a love-relationship with God, it follows that we are utterly dependent on the Holy Spirit for an effective prayer life. As Paul insists, we cannot even call Jesus 'Lord' without the Holy Spirit's enabling.

The Holy Spirit helps us in our weakness

Someone has claimed we shall only ever be beginners when it comes to praying. Deep down, most of us recognize this. Perhaps that is one reason why so many books about prayer line our bookshelves. The good news is that the Holy Spirit, our prayer tutor, not only inspires us to pray, he prays in us and through us, with us and for us. As Paul puts it:

The Spirit himself pleads with God for us in groans that words cannot express.
ROMANS 8:26 (GNB)

The Holy Spirit does not necessarily use words when he prays. Often he uses inarticulate groans and even tears. That is why, when he burdens us to pray for someone in trouble or for a national or international crisis, we may not find words with which to pray. Instead, we might find ourselves weeping, aching inside or groaning or sighing in prayer. This kind of wordless prayer is just as effective as using a language we can understand.

Because it is the Spirit praying in us and through us, and because the Father reads the mind of the Spirit, we can be confident that this non-verbal prayer is heard and understood by the one to whom it is addressed: the Father.

Even our prayers of personal longing which seem like little more than a yearning are signs that the Holy Spirit is praying in us. As Maria Boulding puts it: 'All your love, your stretching out, your hope, your thirst, God is creating in you so that he may fill you. It is not your desire that makes it

A project

Ask yourself what kind of help you need with your prayer. Then ask God's Spirit to help you meet that need.

happen, but his. He longs through your heart... he is on the inside of the longing' (*The Coming of God*, SPCK, 1982, pages 7–8).

FOR REFLECTION

Prayer is the soul's sincere desire,
Uttered or unexpressed,
The motion of a hidden fire
That trembles in the breast.

Prayer is the burden of a sigh,
The falling of a tear,
The upward glancing of an eye,
When none but God is near.

James Montgomery

The Holy Spirit helps us intercede

68

A project

Think of a person or situation about which you are praying. Ask the Holy Spirit to show you what Jesus is praying for in this situation and join in with his prayer.

God has not abandoned us to learn the language of prayer on our own. He has provided us with a teacher-helper: his Holy Spirit. This Holy Spirit lives in us so we can pray anywhere and everywhere and at any time. Because he knows us, he can set us free to be real. And, because he is so close to Christ, he discerns the prayer the great intercessor is expressing in any situation. As Paul puts it:

The Spirit comes to help us, weak as we are. For we do not know how we ought to pray; the Spirit himself pleads with God for us . . . And God, who sees into our hearts, knows what the thought of the Spirit is; because the Spirit pleads with God on behalf of his people and in accordance with his will.

ROMANS 8:26–27 (GNB)

This comes as a great relief to a whole variety of Christians who readily admit that there are occasions when they simply don't know how to pray—like when someone is sick. Should we pray for healing, knowing that God delights to perform miracles or should we pray that the person should be given the strength to endure pain, knowing that pain is sometimes the megaphone through which God speaks to a deaf world? The secret is to discover how Jesus is praying for that person. The writer to the Hebrews reminds us that Jesus is alive and always interceding for us (Hebrews 7:25). It is therefore our responsibility to discover how he is praying in any given situation and to bring our prayer in line with his. If we are praying contrary to the prayer of Jesus we are wasting our time and our breath. The person who can reveal to us the heart and mind and will of Jesus is the Holy Spirit.

A PRAYER

Day by day, O dear Lord, three things I pray
To see Thee more clearly,
Love Thee more dearly,
Follow Thee more nearly,
Day by Day.

After Richard of Chichester

The Holy Spirit changes us

A project

Look back over the road we have travelled together. Remind yourself of the suggestions Jesus made: that we should find a time and a place to pray, that we should come to prayer with high expectations and alertness. And recall what has been written about the role the Holy Spirit plays in the life of prayer. Recognize where you most need help and ask God to send his Spirit to strengthen you.

The Holy Spirit is sometimes likened to water. I was thinking about this imagery while sitting on a shingle beach recently. As I played with the tiny multi-coloured stones at the water's edge, I noticed that, while the dry stones seemed comparatively dull, those washed by the waves lapping the shore shone like jewels and revealed the splendour of their full colours: the greens and browns, blacks and pinks, creams and golds.

Just as water changes dull stones into sparkling gems, so the Holy Spirit changes us. As we observed a few days ago, Paul sums up the work of the Spirit in this way: 'The Spirit produces love, joy, peace, patience, kindness, goodness, faithfulness, humility, and self-control' (Galatians 5:22, GNB).

The love Paul describes means unselfish affection and unceasing activity which benefits the loved one. Joy means the ability to rejoice in spite of difficult places and difficult people. The peace he mentions keeps us serene in the middle of trials. Longsuffering is that quality which helps us to be patient with others. Faithfulness includes a reliability and dependability which never disappoints others or lets them down. Self-control involves living a balanced, disciplined life which is in perfect working order.

This harvest of the Spirit cannot be produced in our own strength. It can be reaped by the Spirit, however. Indeed, this fruit must gradually mature in the life of anyone who claims to be a person of prayer because, as Thomas Merton loved to remind us, 'To pray is to change.' Prayer must never be seen

as a subtle way to change God. Rather prayer must be recognized for what it is—a way in which we are changed into the likeness of Christ and the place where our minds and desires are brought into alignment with his.

A PRAYER

Lord, I know not what I ought to ask of you. You only know what I need. You know me better than I know myself... Teach me to pray. Pray yourself in me.

ARCHBISHOP FRANÇOIS FÉNELON

LISTENING TO THE EXPERT

One of the quickest ways of picking up the correct pronunciation of certain Greek words, I find, is to watch and listen to the locals. I like to watch the position of their tongues as they say certain words, listen to the intonation of their voice and then attempt to imitate them.

If we are to learn the language of prayer, one of the most moving and effective ways is to listen to the Master-pray-er, Jesus himself. In this section, then, we stand on holy ground as we eavesdrop on some of Jesus' own prayers.

Listening to Jesus' trust

One of the things which strikes me every time I meditate on the prayer of Jesus is the frequency with which he uses the word, 'Abba', 'Father'. Like the English word 'Daddy', 'Abba' is one of the first words a Jewish child learns to say.

This term of endearment with which he almost always addressed God is not simply a piece of childish chatter or a deeply personal and familiar pet name, it is a statement of trust.

This was brought home to me when I was swimming in a roof-top swimming pool on one occasion. Sitting on the edge of the pool were two teenage Arab girls dressed in the long skirts they are required to wear. Between them, they were holding their small brother over the water trying to tempt him to have a swim. But the small boy was protesting and making it quite clear that he was not yet ready to be dropped into the water. Just then, his father appeared, whereupon the boy's face lit up. 'Abba! Abba!' he called out excitedly. His father took him into his arms and together they descended into the pool where they played happily together.

Whenever I listen to Jesus using that trusting word, 'Abba', I become aware that I am standing on holy ground. Like his use of that word in the Garden of Gethsemane.

Having asked his disciples to keep watch with him, he took Peter, James and John deeper into the darkness of that garden. There anguish came over him and he admitted that:

'The sorrow in my heart is so great that it almost crushes me.' . . .

He went a little farther on, threw himself face downwards on the ground, and prayed, 'My Father, if it is possible, take this cup of suffering from me! Yet not what I want, but what you want.'

MATTHEW 26:36–39 (GNB)

We hear him uttering a similar cry of trust as he hangs from the cross:

Jesus cried out in a loud voice, 'Father! In your hands I place my spirit!' He said this and died.

LUKE 23:46 (GNB)

What is before us, we know not, whether we shall live or die; but this we know, that all things are ordered and sure. Everything is ordered, with unerring wisdom and unbounded love, by Thee, our God, Who art love. Grant us in all things to see Thy hand; through Jesus Christ our Lord. Amen

Charles Simeon (1759–1836)

A project

Ponder this meditation
by an unknown author
and ask God to enable
you similarly to trust:

My life is but a weaving
Between my God and
me;
I may not choose the
colours,
He knows what they
should be;
For He can view the
pattern
From the upper side
While I can see it only
On this the under side.

Sometimes He weaveth
sorrow,
Which seemeth strange
to me:
But I will trust His
judgement,
And work on faithfully;
'Tis He who fills the
shuttle,
He knows what is best;
So I shall weave in
earnest
And leave with Him the
rest.

At last when life is ended,
With Him I shall abide,
Then I may view the
pattern
Upon the upper side;
Then I shall know the
reason
Why pain with joy
entwined
Was woven in the fabric
Of life that God designed.

Listening to Jesus' dependence

We have observed that, when Jesus addressed God as *Abba*, he was expressing trust in his Father. If we listen carefully, it also becomes apparent that, when he used the word Father, he was also voicing dependence on God. Take John 14:10, for example, where he responds to Philip's request: 'Show us the Father'. As Eugene Peterson praphrases it in *The Message*:

'You've been with me all this time, Philip, and you still don't understand? To see me is to see the Father. So how can you ask, "Where is the Father?" Don't you believe that I am in the Father and the Father is in me? The words that I speak to you aren't mere words. I don't just make them up on my own. The Father who resides in me crafts each word into a divine act. Believe me: I am in my Father and my Father is in me. If you can't believe that, believe what you see—these works.'

Or take John 17:1–2 where he acknowledges that any authority he has is on trust from God. Jesus 'looked up to heaven and said, "Father, the hour has come. Give glory to your Son, so that the Son may give glory to you. For you gave him authority over all mankind, so that he might give eternal life to all those you gave him"' (GNB).

Such humble dependence on God goes against the grain for us because we are sons of Adam and daughters of Eve, born, therefore, with the desire which consumed them—to be as God, even to usurp him. But, if we ask, God will give us the grace gradually to recognize that apart from him we can do nothing and that, what the world needs is not our

A project

Ponder these words which were once displayed in a shop window in America:

'When we depend upon man, we get what men can do.
When we depend upon prayer, we get what God can do.'

Think of occasions when you have depended on God. Reflect on the way he met or helped or inspired you.

impoverished love and compassion but the richness of his love flowing through us. What people need is not the paucity of our wisdom but the incisiveness of his insights and the wealth of his knowledge. And the good news is that, just as Jesus spoke only those words his Father told him to utter and just as Jesus only did those things he saw his Father do, we too can receive guidance from God before we speak or act.

A PRAYER WRITTEN BY DIETRICH BONHOEFFER

O God, early in the morning do I cry unto Thee,
Help me to pray, and to think only of Thee.
I cannot pray alone.
In me there is darkness,
But with Thee there is light.

I am lonely, but Thou leavest me not.
I am feeble in heart, but Thou leavest me not.
I am restless, but with Thee there is peace.
In me there is bitterness,
but with Thee there is patience.

Written at Christmas 1943 while he was awaiting execution in a Nazi concentration camp

Listening to Jesus' childlikeness

My study is full of children—pictures of children that is. There are several pictures of the so-called 'street kids' of Kathmandu: a forlorn little boy fast asleep on the steps of a Buddhist temple, a picture of another small boy dressed only in a sack and yet another of two young girls huddled together under a brightly coloured piece of cloth which covers their almost-naked bodies while they squat on the pavement selling spring onions.

Alongside these pictures which remind me of the children I saw every day when I visited Nepal sit pictures of my namesake in Singapore—a beautiful, well-dressed, wide-eyed child enjoying afternoon tea in one of Singapore's plush hotels. And a picture of my English godchild with her parents and her warmly-clad brothers and sister. As I gaze at 'my' children and pray for them, they remind me that they have one thing in common: they are all dependent on others for their survival. They remind me, too, of a claim Jesus once made:

'I tell you the truth, unless you change and become like little children, you will never enter the kingdom of heaven. Therefore, whoever humbles himself like this child is the greatest in the kingdom of heaven.'

MATTHEW 18:2–4 (NIV)

Jesus not only said this, he showed us how to become childlike in prayer by using that trusting term, 'Father', whenever he addressed God. This word 'Father' was an

A project

Collect some pictures of children—those known to you or strangers. Make a collage or stick them into a scrap book or place them on a notice board in your home. Let their helplessness remind you of your own helplessness before God. Let it give birth to the whispered prayer of trust and dependence: 'Abba! Daddy!'

acknowledgment of his status as God's child. And it was an expression of an attitude—the awareness that he was totally dependent on God for everything—his life, his breath, his survival, power, authority, inspiration, guidance.

Jesus wants us not only to listen to his childlike trust and dependence but to emulate it. He invites us to depend on our heavenly Father for everything: breath and strength, courage and grace, guidance and peace, inspiration and down-to-earth practical provision of our daily needs.

A PRAYER

Ask God to give you the openness of children, to restore to you the gift of wonder and to give you the grace to reach out to him in childlike trust for everything you need.

Listening to Jesus' belovedness

A project

Reflect on this claim:

We are the Beloved. We are intimately loved long before our parents, teachers, spouses, children and friends loved or wounded us. That's the truth of our lives. That's the truth I want you to claim for yourself. That's the truth spoken by the voice [of God] that says, 'You are my Beloved.'

Henri Nouwen *Life of the Beloved*, Hodder and Stoughton, 1992, page 30

When I described the pictures of some of the children which line the walls of my study, I highlighted one of the things these children all had in common—their dependence on others for survival. But just as something unites them, so something divides them. While some of them have enjoyed from conception onwards the security of knowing that they are wanted, loved, cherished and adored, others have never known the committed affection or adoration of anyone. They are orphans or escapees from physical or mental abuse from their families, or fugitives from abject poverty.

Whatever our start in life and no matter how inadequate our parents' loving was, as children of God, our deep-seated need for love can be met. Jesus assures us of this. In fact, he promises that we can be as secure in his love as he was in his Father's love:

'I've loved you the way my Father has loved me. Make yourselves at home in my love. If you keep my commands, you'll remain intimately at home in my love. That's what I've done—kept my Father's commands and made myself at home in his love.'

JOHN 15:9, EUGENE PETERSON'S PARAPHRASE, *THE MESSAGE*

As we listen to Jesus communicating with his Father, it becomes clear that, before the world was made, he had felt secure in his Father's love and this sense of being loved by God had never faded:

'Father, I want those you gave me
To be with me, right where I am,
So they can see my glory, the splendour you gave me,
Having loved me
Long before there ever was a world.'

JOHN 17:24, EUGENE PETERSON'S PARAPHRASE, *THE MESSAGE*

Pray for those who are
seeking to bring the
good news of God's
love to the street kids I
have described. Pray,
too, for yourself that
you may know in your
heart that God loves
you.

Listening to Jesus' maturity

So far, we have been reflecting on the childlikeness with which Jesus related to his Father. We have highlighted the trust and the dependence with which his prayers were laced. But that does not mean that Jesus was childish when he prayed. Unlike many of us, he was never petulant, complaining or clamouring. On the contrary, his relationship with his Father reveals an attractive adult-to-adult maturity and mutuality. Think of the retreat he made on the Mount of Transfiguration, for example. Here we find Jesus enjoying a round-table conference with his Father, with Moses and with Elijah. Luke hints that during this prayer retreat, Jesus consulted with the others about the next lap of his journey to Jerusalem:

[They] talked with Jesus about the way in which he would soon fulfil God's purpose by dying in Jerusalem.

LUKE 9:31 (GNB)

Some painful revelations must have been made during this consultation but we hear of no protest passing Jesus' lips. Instead, he submits to the Father's plan. True submission involves a voluntary donation of everything we have and everything we are. Just as Jesus held his life on an open palm for his Father so the Father donated all his strength and love to his Son so that he might be strengthened for the sacrifice he was to make. Such mutuality is beautiful to behold and inspires the kind of confidence Jesus confessed in the last prayer he prayed before he made his way to Gethsemane:

A project

Meditate on the mutuality which existed between Jesus and his Father. Compare it with adult-to-adult relationships you know of between parents and their grown-up children, and think about the implications of this challenge:

Expect great things from God,
attempt great things for God.

A PRAYER

O Lord, let me not
henceforth desire
health or life, except to
spend them for you,
with you, and in you.
You alone know what is
good for me; do,
therefore, what seems
best. Give to me, or
take from me; conform
my will to yours; and
grant that, with humble
and perfect submission,
and in holy confidence,
I may receive the orders
of your eternal
Providence through
Jesus Christ our Lord.
Amen.

Blaise Pascal (1623–1662)

'Father... All I have is yours, and all you have is mine... you are in me and I am in you.'

JOHN 17:5, 10 (GNB)

Even in Gethsemane where Jesus was brought face to face with the cost to him personally of going to the cross for us, he could pray the prayer of complete submission: 'Not what I want, but what you want' (Mark 14:36).

Listening to Jesus intercede

One of the most moving chapters in the whole of the Bible is John 17 where we have the privilege of listening to Jesus intercede for his disciples. Jesus knows what the disciples do not know—that he is about to die and that, although he will rise again, this night heralds a change in the relationship they had enjoyed with him for the past three years. His love for them is transparent and it gives birth to a cluster of prayers. First, he prays that they may enjoy the kind of oneness with each other which characterized the relationship between the Father and the Son:

'Holy Father! Keep them safe by the power of your name . . . so that they may be one just as you and I are one . . . I pray that they may all be one. Father! May they be in us, just as you are in me and I am in you. May they be one, so that the world will believe that you sent me.'

JOHN 17:11, 21 (GNB)

Or, as Eugene Peterson paraphrases this prayer:

'Holy Father, guard them as they pursue this life
That you conferred as a gift through me,
So that they can be one heart and mind
As we are one heart and mind . . .
The goal is for all of them to become one heart and mind—
Just as you, Father, are in me and I in you.'

This prayer is followed very quickly by a second request:

87

A project

Meditate on the implications of Hebrews 7:25: '[Jesus] always lives to make intercession' (RSV). Recall occasions when you have been in conflict with a fellow believer or a colleague, a friend or a member of your family. Picture Jesus praying for you and for the situation. Or think of a fellowship where Christians are competing with each other and wounding each other rather than loving one another. Picture Jesus praying for that fellowship. Draw alongside him and join him as he continues to pray that they may unite in mind and heart.

'I do not ask you to take them out of the world, but I do ask you to keep them safe from the Evil One.'

JOHN 17:15 (GNB)

There seems to be a clear link between these two prayers which the Church down the ages has been slow to make. Just as in Genesis 3 Satan sidled up to Adam and Eve and put them in touch with their desire to 'be as God', so he continues to lure Christians with the seeming attractions of power. Like Adam and Eve, we fall into his hands and take part in the power struggle which splits churches, wounds individuals and brings dishonour to the name of the One we call Lord. Instead of being nurtured by the sense of oneness which is generated when love flows freely between us and our brothers and sisters in Christ, we fight and criticize our fellow Christians causing the heart of Christ to continue to bleed and causing him to continue to pray that we may live in harmony.

Listening to Jesus praying his goodbyes

We have reflected on some of the requests Jesus made as he prayed for his disciples on the night before he died. One of the reasons why he prayed for them so selflessly was that his prayer was born of compassion.

To have compassion for someone means to suffer with them, to view life through their spectacles or to walk a mile in their moccasins, as the old Indian proverb puts it. In other words, it means to become involved with them.

Because Jesus had compassion for these men with whom he had lived in community for three years, he knew that after his death they would be grief-stricken and guilt-ridden, deeply perplexed and disorientated. As he prayed his goodbyes, he focused, not on himself and his own sense of sorrow and loss but on them and their need for comfort and hope. Consequently, his love for them spilled over into another cluster of prayers. Knowing that, even after the resurrection, joy would only come gradually and fleetingly to these men he loved, he prayed: 'that they might have my joy in their hearts in all its fullness' (John 17:13, GNB).

Aware that, as human beings, we are only truly happy when we are serving and praising God, he makes a further request: 'that they . . . may be truly dedicated to you' (v. 19). Conscious that the secret of fruitfulness lies in oneness with him, he goes on to ask: 'May they be in us, just as you are in me and I am in you' (v. 21). He also keeps their ultimate well-being in mind by praying: 'that they may see my glory' (v. 24). When we compare these prayers with the emotions which

89

A project

Look up John 19:26–27. Listen to Jesus saying goodbye to his mother and to his close friend, John. Meditate, too, on the way he bids farewell to the world: 'Father forgive them, for they do not know what they are doing' (Luke 23:34, NIV). Respond to this prayer in your prayer journal.

weigh us down when we are faced with the sting of impending separation from someone we love deeply, the selflessness with which Jesus intercedes for others shines like a light in a very dark place.

A PRAYER

*Oh Master, grant that I may never seek
So much to be consoled as to console,
To be understood, as to understand,
To be loved as to love with all my soul.*

An adaptation of the prayer of St Francis of Assisi[1]

1. Sebastian Temple,
Fransiscan Communications

THE ONE TO WHOM WE PRAY

As we listen to Jesus praying to his Father, it quickly becomes apparent that he knew that God is love. This inevitably affected the way he prayed.

Several years ago, I discovered that the way we perceive God radically affects our prayer life. I stumbled, too, on the fact that the way we *feel* about God makes a far bigger impact on our prayer than the mental image we have of him. We worship or neglect the 'God of our guts' not the God of our intellect.

I was on retreat when this insight brought me up with a jolt. I had long looked forward to this time alone with God, but as the retreat began I became aware of a curious reluctance to spend leisurely time with him. When I disclosed these feelings to my retreat giver, she suggested that I should spend my first afternoon drawing a picture or a diagram which summed up how I envisaged myself in relationship to God.

The picture which stared up at me horrified me. I had depicted God as a tall, well-built slave driver who was wielding a whip with which he was goading an exhausted me into action. Yet my head knows enough theology to be convinced that God is not a tyrant who thrashes people into obedience. God is love. As I gazed at my caricature of God, I also listened carefully while my head argued with my heart. My mind insisted on quoting the verse 'God is love', but with even greater vehemence my emotions protested that this so-called loving God has many faces—some of them terrifying.

Paying attention to the civil war within helped me to see

why at least one part of me approached this retreat with reticence. When our 'guts' cause the picture of God as tyrant or spoilsport, a Sergeant Major or an overbearing parent to rise before our eyes, we are more likely to withdraw from him rather than to come into his presence offering eager and genuine worship. The experience convinced me that our perception of God makes such a powerful impact on our lives that it merits a regular overhaul.

Maintaining an accurate image of God

There are several ways of ensuring that the picture of God we piece together is as accurate as possible. Paul provides a vital clue when he writes: Jesus 'is the image of the invisible God' (Colossians 1:15, NIV). Since the Son is the 'spitting image' of his Father, it follows that if we know what the Son is like, we also know what the Father is like. We must therefore bring our many images of God alongside the lifestyle, personality and teaching of Jesus. When I did this with my picture of the slave driver, it became patently clear that the God of my guts was not the God of the Gospels. Here we see a rabbi who calls his disciples to spend time with him, live with him and be loved by him *before* he asks them to serve him. When this rabbi's disciples returned from an exhausting mission, he debriefed their experience with them and then, far from goading them into hyperactivity, invited them to 'come away with me and take some rest'. This Rabbi encouraged his disciples into a rhythmical lifestyle where busyness was balanced by rest and

relaxation; where love outpoured was replenished by love absorbed. Jesus was not a slave driver and neither is God.

The origins of some caricatures of God

This realization left me with an uncomfortable question: 'Where had these false feelings about God come from?'

I soon found the answer to that riddle. Projection. For several days prior to the retreat, I had been driving myself. I had worked late into the night to meet publishers' deadlines and deal with correspondence. I had persuaded myself that I could not go away until the desk was clear. In other words, I had been overworking. *I* was the slave driver. Instead of recognizing these tyrannical tendencies as my own, I had projected them on to God, blackening his character and distorting his image.

Other Christians pile different projections on to God. Some do not like themselves very much so they fall into the trap of believing that God doesn't love them either. Others are at best lukewarm towards God and at worst cold towards him, so they are beguiled into believing that God's love for them has grown cold.

There are other reasons why Christians frequently find themselves praying to someone who bears little resemblance to the Jesus of the Gospels. Because we use words like 'father' and 'mother' to describe God, our earthly parents—whether they realize it or not—play a major part in formulating our perception of God. If they have mirrored God's love and parenting in a way that we can sense and feel because it more than meets our need for love, they may have handed to us two vital accurate pieces of the jigsaw. If, however, our father has been, say, harsh or cruel, over-protective or unfair or more absent than present, our view of God may well have been distorted from a very early age. Similarly, if our mother has been over-burdened or over-bearing, rough or neglectful, bad-tempered, irrational or the kind of mother who smothers rather than sets her children free, again our feelings may be feeding us with a false image of God.

School teachers and youth leaders, books, films, hymns and choruses—as well as the prayers we are taught when we are young—also contribute to the picture the word 'God' conjures up in our minds and hearts. Like the small boy of six who was taught the Lord's Prayer: 'Our Father who art in heaven'. 'Where is heaven?' he asked himself. Concluding that heaven was a long way away, he drew the seemingly logical conclusion that this meant that God was the distant, unapproachable one. He lived with this false image of God until he became an adult. One joy-filled day, he realized that God is immanent, always longing that we should draw close to him, always available to us.

Dealing with the distortions

When such moments of revelation come to us, when *we* are shown that our picture of God is inadequate or inaccurate, it is as though we stand at a crossroads. We can either grovel at the cross of Christ in shame and confusion, or we can recognize the moment for what it is: a challenge to change and be changed. There are four steps we can take to ensure that we respond creatively to this challenge.

The first is to confess and repent. By confession, I mean that we simply tell God what he already knows—that we have been praying to a caricature rather than to the real God. By repentance, I mean that we ask God for the grace to respond to the real God who is ready to rescue us; that we also express a longing that our thoughts and emotions may be set free to acknowledge the truth: that God is love.

Next, we need to recognize that this is a graced moment when we are being endowed with the wisdom to view God differently. So the third step is to ask for a further portion of grace so that we are equipped to live a life which revolves around God rather than around self. I find it helpful at such times to pray a prayer which frequently flows from the depths of my heart: 'Lord, turn my whole being to your praise and glory.' Finally, we ask the Holy Spirit to safeguard us from harbouring further false images of God in our heart. We beg him to shine the torchlight of his love on any future inaccurate images which may invade our feelings, and to add to us the grace we need to deal ruthlessly with them.

It is my prayer that, as we look together at the images of God used by Bible writers, our heart-awareness of God may become more pure, more real, more biblical, more trusting— so that our response to the love he offers will always be a loving one and that our relationship with him will deepen over the years rather than deteriorate.

While working through the notes on 'The one to whom we pray', and the images we have of God, I would encourage readers to keep a prayer journal—a notebook in which they record, either in prose or poetry, picture or with colour, their day-by-day responses to the suggestions for reflection. In this way, we can keep track of our unfolding view of God which can, of itself, prompt a paean of praise.

God is love

Yahweh, you examine me and know me,
you know if I am standing or sitting,
you read my thoughts from far away,
whether I walk or lie down, you are watching,
you know every detail of my conduct.

The word is not even on my tongue,
Yahweh, before you know all about it;
close behind and close in front you fence me round,
shielding me with your hand.

PSALM 139:1–5 (JB)

'God loves me so much, he can't take his eyes off me.' That's how one woman responded when she read those verses. It was the kind of response which would have delighted the Psalmist. He, too, relished a deep-down assurance that he was uniquely loved by his Creator. Jesus' close friend, John, believed something similar. He summed up the depth of his feelings in the most succinct and accurate definition of God which has ever been given: 'God is love.'

Not everyone reacts to this psalm in such a positive way, however. Phrases like, 'you examine me' and 'you know every detail of my conduct' send shivers down the spine of some people. They conjure up pictures of God as a policeman or an authoritarian school teacher. Lines like 'you read my thoughts from far away' and 'you fence me in' can feel frightening rather than protective. For some they suggest that God is like the 'Score-card God' John Young describes.[1] This imaginary God allocates a score-card to each human being. On this card he awards ticks for good deeds and crosses for bad deeds. At the end of our lives, he adds up the score. If there are more ticks than crosses, we are safe. If there are more crosses than ticks, we are doomed.

FOR REFLECTION

Re-read the verses from Psalm 139 as slowly as possible until a word or a phrase seems to beg you to stop. Then listen to your heart's reaction. Is the word or the phrase triggering a positive or a negative response? If your response seems to be negative, don't hide it from God. Talk to him about your negativity in the same way as you might talk to a close friend. Ask him to shed light on the source of these feelings. If your response is positive, write or say or sing or draw the prayer which seems to overflow from your heart.

1. John Young, *Our God is Still Too Small*, Hodder and Stoughton, 1988, page 13

God as guide

'We are put on earth for a little space that we may learn to bear the beams of love.' So wrote the poet William Blake. I often reflect on that claim because, as we saw in the previous section, love always streams from the face of God, so this presents us with a challenge: to receive it or reject it. It matters which we choose because, as the Psalmist reminds us, God is our guide:

Where could I go to escape your spirit?
Where could I flee from your presence? . . .
If I flew to the point of sunrise,
or westward across the sea,
your hand would still be guiding me,
your right hand holding me.
PSALM 139:7–10 (JB)

'Your hand would still be guiding me.' That line took on a fresh meaning for me while I was walking in the countryside one day.

Walking down the lane where I used to live, I saw two men clad in walking boots and carrying rucksacks. They were obviously on a ramble but one walked in front of the other like a van towing a car. As they came closer to me, I realized that, like a car being towed, they were linked together—not by a rope but by a white walking stick. The man in front held the pointed end while the man behind held the crook. 'The second man's blind!' I whispered to my husband after the ramblers had passed us. 'Yet, from the look on his face he's

FOR REFLECTION

Ask yourself: 'How have I experienced God's guidance? How has it shaped my life? How would I rate my level of trust today?' Then reflect on another claim of the Psalmist: 'God... will be our guide even to the end' (Psalm 48:14, NIV). Tell God how you feel to have him as your leader.

thoroughly enjoying watching the wonders of creation through his friend's eyes.' This bizarre but beautiful picture seemed to sum up graphically the tremendous trust a person being led must place in the one who is leading. More powerfully than any sermon, it showed me how vital it is that, if we take God as our guide, we trust him implicitly.

A PRAYER

Show me your ways, O Lord,
teach me your paths;
guide me in your truth and teach me,
for you are God my Saviour.

Psalm 25:4–5 (NIV)

A trustworthy guide

The Lord will guide you always;
he will satisfy your needs in a sun-scorched land
and will strengthen your frame.
You will be like a well-watered garden,
like a spring whose waters never fail.
ISAIAH 58:11 (NIV)

I once attended a seminar designed to help Christians in leadership understand how it feels to be led. Seeing the blind man I mentioned in 'God as guide' reminded me of one of the exercises we were encouraged to participate in.

We were divided into pairs and asked to call one person A and the other B. Partner A was to blindfold partner B, making sure that they could see nothing, and then take them for a walk around the nearby university grounds.

I was A so I blindfolded my partner, took her by the hand, led her from the church hall where we were meeting and out along the street towards the university campus. At first I could feel fear flowing through her fingers, but gradually as I tried to help her to anticipate what was coming with comments like, 'There's a kerb here', or, 'We're approaching a lamp post', I felt her relax and I knew her trust in me was growing. That was the stage when she began to express to me the emotions which were vying for attention inside her. When, eventually, we arrived back at the church hall, she told me how terrified she had been at first but how, as time passed and trust blossomed, she felt a bonding developing between us.

FOR REFLECTION

Is your God dull, a scowling spoilsport, someone you can trust, someone who has your best interests at heart or...? Be honest with God about the way you feel about him.

Journeying through life with God can feel rather like travelling blindfold at times and if we are to bond with him rather than recoil in fear and dread, we need to keep the lines of communication open and honest. One Christian who failed to do this admitted that, as a young man, he had concluded 'that God was a bit of a spoilsport frowning on anything that was enjoyable and promoting anything that hurt or was dull.'[1]

Today's verse from Isaiah assures us that God is not like that but our hearts may contradict the prophet's words.

1. Ian Petit, *The God Who Speaks*, DLT, 1989, page 11

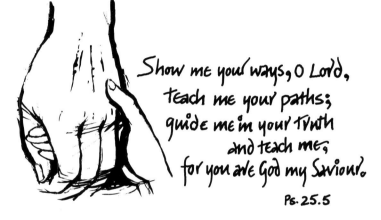

Show me your ways, O Lord,
teach me your paths;
guide me in your truth
and teach me;
for you are God my Saviour.

Ps. 25.5

God as instructor

In 'God as guide' and 'A trustworthy guide' we have observed that sometimes we stumble through life as though we were blind. At other times, life seems much more spacious and God's guidance comes in the form of spontaneous instruction rather than step-by-step leading.

I was thinking about this one morning while my husband and I were swimming near our home. I had swum to a small secluded cove and I was watching my husband skim through the water on his back. As he approached a jagged rock near me, I cried out: 'There's a rock just behind you.' Whereupon he slowed down, continued to enjoy the buoyancy of the water, the warmth of the sun and the beauty of the beach.

My reaction reminded me of a promise we find in Isaiah: 'Whether you turn to the right or to the left, your ears will hear a voice behind you, saying, "This is the way; walk in it"' (Isaiah 30:19–21, NIV). The picture here is not of someone groping through life clinging anxiously or even trustingly to a white stick, incapable of making personal choices. It is of someone enjoying life in all its fulness; journeying through life energetically. Most of the time, because their life is centred on God, the choices they make are wise. Every now and again, they hesitate, not knowing which road to take or which choice to make. When they contemplate making a wrong choice, the God who loves them calls: 'This is the way.' They know God well enough to accept that he is not wanting to cramp their style but rather to promote their well-being. In Jesus we see someone who models this freedom perfectly. Like a horse carrying a skilful rider, Jesus canters through life with obvious joy. From time to time, however, he pauses, sensitive to the slightest tug at the reins his heavenly rider makes.

Some Christians cannot conceive of God as a reliable guide. For them, God is the 'Grand Old Man' in the skies. They treat him with respect but because the word 'old' carries the connotation 'old fashioned' or irrelevant, they assume that this God cannot be expected to involve himself with twentieth-century problems like mortgages and car purchasing, faxes and form-filling. He is totally 'other'. Irrelevant.

God as maker

Come, let us bow down in worship,
let us kneel before the Lord our Maker;
for he is our God.
PSALM 95:6 (NIV)

I sometimes pray with clay. By this, I mean that, while holding
a lump of clay in my hand, I meditate on God's description of
himself as a potter and of us as clay (see, for example, Isaiah
64:8; Jeremiah 18:6) and at the same time pommel and press
and push and pull until the hard lump gradually yields to the
warmth of my palms and the strength of my fingers.

Whenever I do this, I am reminded that in some strange,
inexplicable way, the thing which we create becomes an
extension of ourselves so that, even though the end product
may be far from perfect, we feel an attachment to it and a
reluctance to part from it.

Perhaps that is why a particular statue in Chartres
Cathedral, of God creating Adam, never never fails to move
me. As God puts the finishing touches to the man he is
making, tenderness seems to stream from his entire being
causing a blissful, contented smile to light up Adam's face.

Henri Nouwen helps us to enter into the mystery of what
it means to be a creature in relationship with our Creator:

From all eternity, long before you were born and became a part of
history, you existed in God's heart... The eyes of love had seen
you as precious, as of infinite beauty, as of eternal value... Long

before any human being saw us, we are seen by God's loving eyes. Long before anyone heard us cry or laugh, we are heard by our God who is all ears for us. Long before any person spoke to us in this world, we are spoken to by the voice of eternal love. Our preciousness, uniqueness and individuality are not given to us by those who meet us in clock-time . . . but by the One who has chosen us with an everlasting love, a love that existed from all eternity and will last through all eternity.[1]

FOR REFLECTION

Re-read Henri Nouwen's claim. Try to drink in its implications. Listen carefully to your heart's response and talk to God about it. Then, if you can, echo the Psalmist's prayer:
I praise you because I am fearfully and wonderfully made;
your works are wonderful.

Psalm 139:14

1. Henri Nouwen, *Life of the Beloved*, Hodder and Stoughton, 1993, page 49

God as comforting mother

In 'God as maker' I described the 'Creation of Adam' statue and the tenderness which seems to stream from God's face and flow through his fingers as he puts the finishing touches to the first man he made.

That word 'tenderness' reminds me of another of the Bible's images of God—God as a comforting mother:

As a mother comforts her child,
so will I comfort you.

ISAIAH 66:13 (NIV)

Isaiah reveals the nature of the comfort referred to here. It includes the intimacy and nurture involved whenever a caring mother breast-feeds her baby:

For you will nurse and be satisfied
at her comforting breasts:
you will drink deeply and delight in her overflowing abundance...
you will nurse and be carried on her arm
and dandled on her knees.

ISAIAH 66:11–12 (NIV)

The Psalmist appears to have enjoyed this kind of relationship with God. He once testified:

My heart has no lofty ambitions...
Enough for me to keep my soul tranquil and quiet
like a child in its mother's arms,
as content as a child that has been weaned.

PSALM 131:1–2 (JB)

Carlo Carretto clearly enjoyed this kind of relationship. He wrote: 'In God I feel like a child in its mother's lap.'[1]

Delia Smith suggests that when prayer becomes the place where we develop a relationship with God as mother, tenderness can touch the deepest level of our being. That is my personal experience. She also suggests that, 'just as a baby whose eyes are tightly closed suckles instinctively at the breast, so we are unknowingly embraced and nurtured throughout the whole of our lives'.[2]

Because of their relationship with their earthly mother, some Christians recoil from the Bible's use of this imagery. Envisaging God as mother conjures up a picture of someone unyielding or smothering, someone who is too over-burdened or inhibited to give the kind of bodily comfort described here. This imagery can bring healing to such people when they realize that long before our earthly parents even saw us on a scan, God was gazing on us with great tenderness and nursing and feeding us in the way Isaiah describes.

Listen to your heart's response to this picture of God as mother. Turn this response into a prayer.

1. Carlo Carretto, *Love is for Living*, DLT, 1976, page 19

2. Delia Smith, *Journey Into God*, Hodder and Stoughton, 1988, page 57

Keep my soul tranquil & quiet
like a child in its mother's arms.

Ps. 131

God as midwife

We have observed that even before our earthly parents saw us, God was at work in our lives. The Psalmist was so overwhelmed by this that he described God as a midwife:

You drew me out of the womb,
you entrusted me to my mother's breasts;
placed on your lap from my birth,
from my mother's womb you have been my God.

PSALM 22:9–10 (JB)

Delia Smith claims that God is much more than a midwife. She describes earthly mothers as 'spiritual surrogates' suggesting they were created because God could not be everywhere at once. She calls God 'our truest and closest mother.'[1]

The Psalmist, too, sees God as more than a midwife. He paints a beautiful picture of God as provider suggesting that from the moment of conception we were known, understood, cherished:

It was you who created my inmost self,
and put me together in my mother's womb;
for all these mysteries I thank you:
for the wonder of myself, for the wonder of your works.
You know me through and through,
from having watched my bones take shape
when I was being formed in secret,
knitted together in the limbo of the womb.

PSALM 139:13–15 (JB)

Re-read the Psalmist's claims. Turn them over and over in your mind letting their implications impress themselves on your heart. Then consider the claim that the song makes: 'He's got the whole world in his hands ... He's got you and me in his hands.'

From the moment of conception we were fed, first through our mother's bloodstream via the placenta and then, after we were born, through the milk which flowed from her breasts. We were also cushioned by the fluid in the womb which surrounded and supported us. Wherever our mother carried us, hidden inside her body we were safe, secure and always living, moving, having our being, growing.

The challenge comes to us as Christian adults to learn to receive the beams of intimate love which always stream from the tender one to us. For many of us this is hard because of the picture of God we have pieced together throughout our lives. Like the man I spoke to while I was writing these notes who thinks of God as a Sergeant Major whose one aim in life is not to love us but to bark at us until we obey his commandments.

1. Delia Smith, *Journey Into God*, Hodder and Stoughton, 1988, page 57

God as Father

'Your thoughts of God are too human,' said Martin Luther to
Erasmus. The same could be said of many of us. Like those
who believe God to be like a Managing Director.

These people, constructing a mental picture of God from
their experience of life, picture him as a magnified human
being. They know that when a person is placed in charge of
thousands of people that person can no longer even attempt
to know or care individually for those in their care. They
therefore conclude that since God assumes responsibility for
everyone in the world, contact with infinitesimal individuals
becomes impossible. The thought that God can hear and
answer the prayers and hopes of people all over the world
seems laughable because their image of God is of a 'harassed
telephone operator answering callers at a switchboard of
superhuman size'.[1]

They insist: 'The God who is responsible for the terrifying
vastness of the universe cannot possibly be interested in the
lives of the minute specks of consciousness which exist on
this insignificant planet.'[2]

These pictures of God are a far cry from the biblical images
which suggest that God is inviting us to enjoy an intimate,
emotional relationship with him—a relationship where we, the
loved one, can look to him, the initiator of the love, at any time
and in any place and rest assured that he is taking full responsibility for our well being. Like the picture Jesus paints of God as a
perfect Father: 'When you pray, say: "Father"' (Luke 11:1, NIV).
Or like the picture of God as parent painted by Hosea:

When Israel was a child I loved him, and I called [him] ... I myself taught Ephraim to walk, I took them in my arms ... I led them with reins of kindness, with leading-strings of love. I was like someone who lifts an infant close against his cheek; stooping down to him I gave him his food ... Ephraim, how could I part with you? Israel, how could I give you up? ... My heart recoils from it, my whole being trembles at the thought ... for I am God, not man.

HOSEA 11:1–4, 7–9 (JB)

Read the passage from Hosea as slowly as possible. Replace the words 'Israel' and 'Ephraim' with your own name. Notice how you respond and record your feelings in your journal.

1. J.B. Phillips, *Your God is Too Small*, pages 41–42

2. Ibid., page 40

God as a regal Father

We have homed in on the biblical image of God as 'Father'. But, as J.B. Phillips rightly pointed out, when Jesus encouraged us to call God '*Abba*', 'Daddy', he was not inviting us to crawl through life in spiritual rompers or to remain infantile in our relationship. He himself modelled an adult-to-adult relationship with God as well as revealing to us what his Father is really like.

Four words sum up Jesus' relationship with his Father: submission, mutuality, partnership and consultation. Submission means a voluntarily donation of everything we have and everything we are. Jesus' motto was: 'Not my will, but yours be done.' The mutuality which existed between them is clearly seen in the way they loved each other. Love flowed from the Father to the Son on public occasions like his baptism and the transfiguration: 'This is my own dear Son, with whom I am pleased' (Matthew 17:5, GNB). And, from the way Jesus spoke of his Father, this love was clearly reciprocated: 'The world must learn that I love the Father' (John 14:31, NIV). Jesus also emphasizes that he not only consulted his Father in everything, but he and the Father were partners: 'the Father loves the Son and shows him all that he himself is doing' (John 5:20, GNB).

Jesus not only himself enjoyed a rich relationship with his regal Father, he encourages us to believe that we can enjoy a similar relationship. Through a story (Luke 15:11–32) he underlines that, when he uses the word 'Father', he is not inviting us to base our image of God on earthly fathers known to us, some of whom may be authoritarian or tyrannical, indulgent or neglectful, cruel or over-protective. *His* Father is all-loving and compassionate, gentle, kind, patient and forgiving; willing to suffer rejection and abandonment, always eager for reconciliation whenever there is a rift in the relationship and creative in finding ways of demonstrating his unending love. This Father is also majestic—the God of the Psalmist: 'The Lord reigns, he is robed in majesty' (Psalm 93:1, NIV).

The word majestic comes from the Latin meaning 'greatness'. While Jesus enjoyed intimacy with his Father, he never lost sight of his splendour and magnificence. He invites us to enter to the full into the depths of the Father's love but always to remember that our Father is kingly, 'other', great.

FOR REFLECTION

To me, God is like
....
When I reflect on God as Father I feel
....

God as passionate lover

Someone who is obsessed with us. That is how the Bible describes God. The Old Testament prophets portray him as a passionate lover and this theme is personified in Jesus—particularly in his relationships with his disciples.

The prophet Isaiah is one who was entrusted with broadcasting the marvel of God's incomprehensible love. He is one who publishes the good news that God is the lover absolute; that we, God's creatures, may know that our whole being can be immersed in the ocean of the Creator's love which he likens to the love a bridegroom has for his bride:

As a bridegroom rejoices over his bride,
so will your God rejoice over you.
ISAIAH 62:5 (NIV)

Jesus embodies this mysterious love. His passion for his disciples is particularly marked at the Last Supper when he publicly prays his pain-filled goodbyes: 'He had always loved those who were his in the world, but now he showed how perfect his love was . . .' (John 13:1). First he served them by washing their dirty, sweaty, sandy feet, then he expressed his longing that their separation should be as short as possible:

'There are many rooms in my Father's house . . .
I am going now to prepare a place for you,
and after I have gone and prepared you a place,
I shall return to take you with me;
so that where I am you may be too.'
JOHN 14:1–2

He goes on to plead with his Father that 'they may be one
in us'. His language is reminiscent of the love-language
used in the Song of Songs:

My Beloved is mine and I am his . . . and the banner he raises
over me is love.
SONG OF SONGS 2:16, 3

People ravished by such loving relationships find
themselves re-energized, changed, set free to enjoy
beauty, creativity and life in all its fullness. Yet many
Christians seem to live cramped, narrow, joyless lives.
They are less colourful and creative than their pagan
counterparts. Often this is because they have never
encountered God as a passionate lover and pray instead
to a cantankerous, jealous, spoilsport God who schemes
only to squeeze them into a spiritual strait-jacket.

FOR REFLECTION

Jesus once asked his disciples the question: 'Who do you say I am?'
(Mark 8:29, NIV) Would your answer include: 'You are our heavenly
Bridegroom?' (see Revelation 19:7). If so, are we acting as his fiancée?

You are my friends — if you do

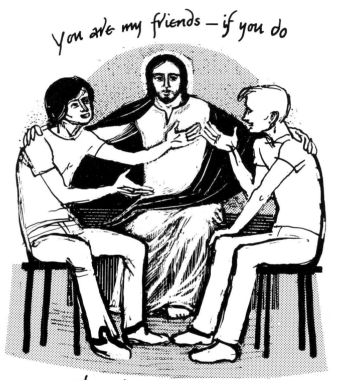

what I command you.

Jn. 15.14

God as friend

God is the eternal, pursuing lover who takes the initiative—falling in love with us and loving us infinitely. According to the Bible he is also the divine friend.

In Exodus, for example, we see God forging a firm friendship with Moses: 'The Lord would speak to Moses face to face, as a man speaks with his friend' (Exodus 33:11, NIV). 'A friend loves at all times.' 'A friend . . . sticks closer than a brother.' 'Wounds from a friend can be trusted,' claims the author of Proverbs (17:17; 18:24; 27:6, NIV).

This is the kind of friendship Jesus enfleshes. He loves his disciples even when they misunderstand and misinterpret his mission and message. He loves them when they deny and abandon him. He continues to offer them patient love when each of them is riddled with doubt after the resurrection. Take his befriending of Thomas, for example.

Thomas refused to believe that Jesus had appeared to the others. He protested that he would not believe unless he could see the holes the nails had made in Jesus' hands and put his hands into Jesus' wounded side.

Eight days later . . . Jesus came in and and stood among them . . . He spoke to Thomas, 'Put your finger here; look, here are my hands. Give me your hand; put it into my side.'
JOHN 20:26–27 (JB)

This act of friendship drew praise and a profound statement of faith from Thomas: 'My Lord and my God!'

But the quality of Jesus' friendship was such that he was unafraid to confront when necessary. So gently he challenges Thomas: 'Stop your doubting, and believe!' (John 20:27, GNB). Similarly, before his death he wounds all of his disciples with his warning: 'This very night all of you will run away and leave me.' Peter protests: 'I will never leave you, even though all the rest do!' And Jesus confronts and exposes his fickleness: 'Before the cock crows tonight, you will say three times that you do not know me' (Matthew 26:31, 33–34, GNB). Faithful, undeserved, unconditional, confrontational love. That is the kind of friendship love we may expect from God.

FOR REFLECTION

Think of times in your life when you have been conscious of the friendship of God. Relive the memories. Thank God for them. Ask yourself: Am I relating to him today as the friend with whom I can share anything and everything? If not, why not?

God as life-changing friend

When someone believes in us and stays alongside us like the 'friend who sticks closer than a brother' (Proverbs 18:24, NIV), they begin to transform our lives by drawing out our full potential. Even when we display little confidence in ourselves, they go on believing in us. Jesus did this for his disciples.

Think of the changes which took place in Peter's life, for example. When he first met Jesus, he was conscious only of his own unworthiness: 'He fell on his knees before Jesus and said, "Go away from me, Lord! I am a sinful man!" ' (Luke 5:8, GNB). At this time, Peter's name was 'Simon son of Jonah' (Matthew 16:17, NIV). Now Jesus re-names him: 'You are Peter' (Matthew 16:18, NIV).

In Greek, the word Peter means 'rock' or 'rock-like'. It was carefully chosen by Jesus to symbolize the changes which would take place in Peter as his leadership qualities developed. There were to be times when Peter appeared to be anything but rock-like, yet Jesus continued to have confidence in him, to develop his leadership skills, to pray for him, to stay alongside him and even to restore him when he failed (see John 21). Consequently, on the Day of Pentecost, we see Jesus' prophecy being fulfilled as Peter assumes the leadership of the infant church.

As we saw in the introduction to this section of the book, Paul describes Jesus as the 'exact likeness' of his Father. In other words, the life-changing friendship Jesus offered to Peter and the other disciples is also offered to us by God. This is good news for Christians whose perception of God is outgrown or inaccurate—like those who feel that God stifles creativity and clamps down on any form of enjoyment. Or like those who equate God with their conscience: that still, small voice which nags at them and makes them feel guilty whenever they contemplate any kind of wrongdoing or fail in any way; that voice which condemns and crushes them after they have put a foot wrong and even, sometimes, when they have done nothing amiss.

FOR REFLECTION

Ask yourself: 'Does God as I know him draw out my full potential or does the "God of my guts" diminish me?'

God as companion

'Prayer is a cumulative life of friendship with God,' claimed H.E. Fosdick. God is not simply a friend but a companion. The word companion comes from two Latin words: *cum* (with) and *panis* (bread). It literally means to break bread with, to accompany, to go hand in hand, to be coupled with. In other words a companion is one who journeys alongside us.

Almost as soon as he began his public ministry, Jesus made it clear that he wanted companions—people with whom he could live in community. Those who would accompany him in times of turmoil as well as in times of joy, when relaxing as well as when working. He invited twelve men first to be his companions and only second to become co-workers in ushering in his kingdom.

His relationships with these men are illuminating. They accompanied him in moments of intense joy—like when he was praying and while he was being transfigured on the mountain. They were also alongside him when he was most vulnerable—in the Garden of Gethsemane. There he begged them to stay with him, to alleviate his aloneness, which is part of the purpose of companionship. As he explained to them: 'The sorrow in my heart is so great that it almost crushes me. Stay here and keep watch with me' (Matthew 26:38, GNB).

On the first Easter Day, we find Jesus drawing alongside two of his bewildered, disillusioned friends. As these two trudged to Emmaus, while they discussed Jesus' crucifixion and tales of his resurrection: 'Jesus himself drew near and walked along with them' (Luke 24:15, GNB).

Having shed light on the events which had left them so battered and bemused, Jesus continued to offer them companionship—quite literally. He made himself known as he broke bread at their table.

The implication is that God will never leave us or forsake us. He journeys with us wherever we go and he yearns that we should spend quality time with him.

FOR REFLECTION

When do you find it easiest to be conscious of the companionship God offers? When is it most difficult? Talk to God about that. Then, find a few quiet moments when you can look back over the things you have written about your perception of God in your prayer journal and go on asking him for the grace to see him more clearly.

PRAYER WHEN THINGS ARE TOUGH

When we were listening to Jesus pray, we heard him beg God to give unity to Christians all over the world and down the ages. Sadly, because of our innate self-centredness, we do not always enjoy the harmony for which Jesus prayed. In fact, we often experience the opposite: conflict instead of peace. This does not mean that we should stop praying. It does mean that we need to learn to pray when things are tough—particularly when we are locked in conflict with others.

Different people cope with conflict in different ways. This was highlighted for me when I read a few verses from the Acts of the Apostles to a group of Christians on one occasion. The verses I read came from Acts 15 where we read of Paul and Barnabas' thrilling missionary tour and its aftermath:

Some time later Paul said to Barnabas, 'Let us go back and visit the brothers in all the towns where we preached the word of the Lord and see how they are doing.' Barnabas wanted to take John, also called Mark, with them, but Paul did not think it wise to take him, because he had deserted them in Pamphylia and had not continued with them in the work. They had such a sharp disagreement that they parted company. *Barnabas took Mark and sailed for Cyprus, but Paul chose Silas and left, commended by the brothers to the grace of the Lord. He went through Syria and Cilicia, strengthening the brothers.*

ACTS 15:36–41 (NIV, EMPHASIS MINE)

'How do you feel about Paul and Barnabas as you reflect on these verses?' I asked the group.

O Lord,
remember those of ill will.
But do not remember all the suffering they inflicted on us,
remember the fruits we have bought,
thanks to our suffering—
our comradeship, our loyalty,
our humility, our courage,
our generosity,
the greatness of heart which has grown out of all this . . .

(Found scribbled on a piece of paper near the body of a dead child at Ravensbruck camp where 92,000 women and children died.)

In response, some admitted that they felt disappointed that two such fine men of God should be locked in conflict. Others confessed to feeling angry with the two missionaries. Yet others expressed feelings of relief that two people who were so evidently used by God could display the same kind of weaknesses and prejudices many of us struggle with. Some voiced feelings of despair: 'If people like Paul and Barnabas couldn't sort out their differences, what chance do we have?' And some of the group said they felt bewildered and confused by this apparently unresolved tension. 'Surely, these two who so clearly walked close to God should have been able to resolve their differences?' they challenged.

The effects of conflict

Conflict between Christians still bewilders some and crushes, wounds and divides others. It frequently engenders fear and guilt—especially in circles where Christians have been taught to expect that friction, of itself, is wrong, that it will never invade their fellowship. Yet the fact of the matter is that conflict continues to afflict contemporary Christians. It disrupts marriages, even Christian ones. It batters friendships, fellowships and families. It causes havoc in committees, leaving behind it a trail of destruction, loneliness, misunderstanding and deep-seated hurt and bewilderment.

Because conflict often creeps up on us suddenly, like a storm blowing in from the sea on a summer's day, it almost always takes us by surprise so we rarely prepare for it. Yet most people, without realizing it, establish ways of coping with it.

Three ways of coping with conflict: fight, flight, freeze

Some fight every step of the way. So if conflict erupts in the home, at work or at church, they roll up their emotional sleeves and become embroiled. If they had been present when Paul and Barnabas had their sharp disagreement, they would have entered the fray and tried to sort out the situation—taking sides if necessary. Others cannot cope with conflict so if they had been present when Paul and Barnabas separated, they would have run away or buried their heads in the proverbial sand—pretending nothing was happening to spoil the unity of the fellowship. Yet others are paralysed by tension of any kind. When it rears its head, they freeze and become powerless.

Fight, flight or freeze. It is important that we recognize which of these reactions we adopt when tensions arise in our life, because it may be determining the way we relate to people at work or at home, at church or socially.

Those who take fright or freeze, for example, may manipulate their relationships in such a way that they become conflict-excluders or conflict-avoiders. That is, they make it almost impossible for conflict to erupt by setting firm boundaries between themselves and others. A conflict-excluder speaks in an authoritarian 'don't you dare contradict me' voice or uses conversation-stopper phrases like 'the Bible says' with the tone of voice which is designed to prevent anyone challenging their perception or viewpoint. That is why, in the diagram below, the conflict-excluder looks bigger than the person with whom he or she is attempting to relate.

The conflict-avoider appears to be easier to relate to because he or she does not lord it over others in the same way as the conflict-excluder. Yet, as the diagram clearly shows, conflict-avoiders also erect barriers between themselves and others. Their way of doing this is to avoid discussing controversial subjects—like politics or forms of worship. This way, they keep their relationships sweet but the scope of their conversation is extremely limited and forming close relationships with them is far from easy.

Conflict-excluding

The conflict-excluder appears bigger than others even though physically (s)he may be the same size.

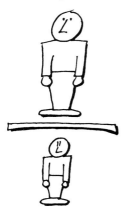

Those whose initial reaction is to fight often take pride in the fact that, for them, conflict is, at least, resolved. They may allow their tempers to boil over, but having expressed their feelings, they cool down again fairly quickly. But the question needs to be asked: 'How many people have I wounded with my words while the pot of my anger was boiling over?' And another: 'Have I allowed myself to fall into the kind of trap Satan set for Adam and Eve in Genesis 3?'

In Genesis 3 we see Satan setting husband and wife against each other so that they blame and accuse each other in a cruel and unkind way. The fighters can quickly find themselves causing irrevocable harm with the lava of their words even though this was never their intention.

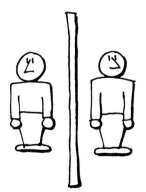

Conflict-avoiding

These two are the same size but there is still a barrier between them.

Blessed are the peacemakers.

Coping the kingdom way

There is an alternative reaction if we are to believe the Gospels. It is made by Jesus. If we observe it, we need become neither conflict-excluders nor conflict-avoiders. We need resort neither to fighting, freezing or fleeing. Instead, we can view conflict differently, recognizing it for what it is—the potential for growth; the ground where seeds of understanding may be sown so that, in time, the fruits of reconciliation will be reaped. For Jesus challenges us to become conflict-resolving people—to use his own term, to become 'peacemakers':

'You are in the right place when you make peace because you will be filled with a joy which cannot be dented', he claims in Matthew 5:9 (my interpretation of 'blessed are the peacemakers'). Later, he fleshes out this teaching with a vivid pen picture. 'Imagine that you have wronged God,' he suggests, 'and you decide to put things right. You come to the temple, walk through the Court of the Gentiles, the Court of the Women, the Court of the Men and eventually reach the threshold of the Court of the Priests. There, you stand at the rail and just as you are about to hand over to the priest the sin-offering you have brought, you remember things are not right between you and your brother. Leave your gift there in front of the altar. Go and make peace with your brother and then come back and offer your gift to God. You cannot be right with God until your relationships with others are right' (my interpretation of Matthew 5:23).

Jesus' view of conflict

In other words, Jesus sees conflict as an inevitable part of being human, as homework to be done and as a life-changing friend who warns us that all is not well. He views it as a sign that things need to change—that *we* need to change.

With this in mind, we shall meditate on some of the suggestions he makes for handling sensitive relationships. I trust that, as a result of these meditations, conflict will no longer dismay, disappoint or frustrate us but rather excite us as we sense its potential for good, for healing and for long-lasting reconciliation and growth.

Blessed are the peacemakers: conflict-resolving people.

Don't play tit-for-tat

When someone has hurt or offended us, the natural reaction is to retaliate—either to find some way of paying them back or to punish them by withdrawing our love. After all, the oldest law in the world clearly states that if there is serious injury, you are to take 'life for life, eye for eye, tooth for tooth, hand for hand, foot for foot, burn for burn, wound for wound, bruise for bruise' (Deuteronomy 19:21).

Yet Jesus sweeps aside this law and replaces it with a much more demanding counter-suggestion: 'You have heard that it was said, "An eye for an eye, and a tooth for a tooth." But now I tell you: do not take revenge on someone who wrongs you' (Matthew 5:38, GNB). And he paints a powerful pen-picture to illustrate his point: 'If anyone slaps you on the right cheek, let him slap your left cheek too' (Matthew 5:39, GNB).

It is not uncommon for Christians to mock this piece of teaching simply because they have not placed it in its cultural context and have therefore not fully understood its far-reaching implications.

Jesus is encouraging his listeners to imagine that a right-handed man has slapped another on the right cheek. The only way he can do this with ease is to slap the victim with the *back* of his hand. But the Jewish law claimed that hitting someone with the back of the hand was twice as insulting as slapping with the flat of the hand. So Jesus' listeners would have known that he was implying a principle which extended far beyond face-slapping; that he was saying, in effect: 'Even if someone deliberately hurts or insults you, don't retaliate, or play tit-for-tat. Don't even allow seeds of resentment to take root in you. Instead, accept the pain and the insult and react in a revolutionary way: by remembering to love your would-be enemy and to pray for your persecutors' (Matthew 5:43).

FOOD FOR THOUGHT

Is there someone in your church or at work or in your neighbourhood who clearly does not like you and who seems to plot to bring about your downfall? Imagine what might happen if you acted on Jesus' suggestions. To love those who show us no love is the most effective way of proving that God's Spirit is at work in you.

Love your enemies

We have observed how Jesus swept from our path the law of tit-for-tat and replaced it with that most demanding challenge anyone has ever given: 'Love your enemies, do good to those who hate you, bless those who curse you' (Luke 6:27–28, NIV). Now, we tease out the implications of this seemingly impossible demand.

In English, we use the word 'love' to describe a whole variety of emotions: the affection which flows between mother and child, the passionate feelings which consume lovers, the warmth a person feels for their closest friend and the goodwill with which we relate to acquaintances, colleagues and others.

In Greek, there are four separate words to differentiate between these four kinds of loving. The word Jesus uses when he says, 'Love your enemies', is *agape* which means unfailing benevolence and never-ending goodwill. As William Barclay once put it: 'If we regard a person with *agape*, it means that no matter what that person does to us, no matter how he treats us, no matter if he insults us or injures us or grieves us, we will never allow any bitterness against him to invade our hearts, but will regard him with that unconquerable benevolence and goodwill which will seek nothing but his highest good.'[1]

In other words, Jesus is not asking us to fall in love with those who have hurt or offended us, nor to love them with the same kind of affection we feel for some members of our family. He is inviting us to love from the will and the mind rather than the heart. He is begging for sacrifice not sentiment:

142 **AN EXAMPLE**

From the cross, Jesus saw the disciples who had deserted him when he needed them, as well as his tormentors, and he prayed: 'Father forgive ... Father forgive ... Father forgive.'

the determination on our part to help those who would harm us; to find practical ways of enriching the lives of those who do not like us and whom we may not necessarily like or count among our friends.

A PRAYER

*Fill me, Lord, with your grace
That I may achieve the unachievable,
To love as you love.*

1. William Barclay, *The Gospel of Matthew*, volume 1, The Saint Andrew Press, pages 173–74

Pray for your persecutors

It takes courage and strength to act on the teaching we have examined so far: Jesus' suggestion that we refuse to take revenge when people hurt or offend us and that we should love such people. It takes courage and strength, too, to embody his further challenge: 'Pray for those who persecute you' (Matthew 5:44, NIV). For, once again, Jesus is begging us to swim against the tide of human nature.

Ever since the Fall people have bickered: accusing and blaming one another when relationships go awry. But if Jesus is to be believed, it need not be like this. According to him hurting and potentially hateful experiences can become healing ones through the medium of prayer. In fact prayer is the key to coping with conflict in a Christlike way. We shall never be able to live the Jesus-way in our own strength. We need God's grace to equip us for a seemingly impossible task. It is through prayer that we receive this much-needed grace.

There are other reasons why we should pray for our persecutors. To intercede for someone in the way Jesus suggests means to come into God's presence with this person on our heart. In this instance, to stand before God with our potential enemy on our heart. It is impossible to linger in the presence of God and remain full of hatred, bitterness and resentment. So such prayer, among other things, will change us even when it does nothing to change our persecutors or the situation in which we find ourselves. To pray is to change.

When we pray in this way, we need to remind ourselves that Jesus himself is already praying for us and the person with whom we are at variance. It follows that, if our prayer is to be effective, we must echo this prayer of Jesus for the situation, not one which runs counter to the prayer springing from his heart. This way we bring ourselves and our desires into line with him.

Another reason why we should pray for our persecutors is that such prayer automatically strengthens the *agape* love we have been thinking about. To pray, then, paves the way to loving others as Jesus loves us.

FOOD FOR THOUGHT

Is there someone or a group of people who have hurt or offended you? Have you been harbouring resentment or bitterness, saying, perhaps: 'I'll never forgive them for that'? Or have you been punishing them? Talk to Jesus about the situation. Ask him to heal the hurts inside you and to give you the desire and the grace to do what he did on the cross—to forgive.

Forgive

We have observed how Jesus practised what he preached by praying for his enemies from his cross. The prayer he prayed is an important one: 'Father forgive them' (Luke 23:34). The Greek suggests that he did not merely pray this prayer once but that he repeated it over and over again.

And he encourages us similarly to forgive, explaining that 'if you forgive men when they sin against you, your heavenly Father will also forgive you. But if you do not forgive men their sins, your Father will not forgive your sins' (Matthew 6:14–15, NIV). He also exhorts us to go on and on forgiving, so when Peter asked him, 'Lord, how many times shall I forgive my brother when he sins against me? Up to seven times?' Jesus answers: 'Not seven times, but seventy-seven times' (Matthew 18:21, NIV). These are hard sayings, so we will now turn to teasing out what forgiveness entails.

Forgiveness does not start with forgetting. Just as, on the cross, Jesus was acutely aware of those who had wronged him and of the physical and emotional pain torturing him, so true, authentic, costly forgiveness begins with remembering as vividly as possible the incident which has hurt or offended us. When we are in touch with our innermost pain, we know what and who it is that we have to forgive.

Such knowledge faces us with a choice: to play tit-for-tat, recognizing that there is a sense in which this is our right. As the ancient law we've looked at puts it: 'an eye for an eye and a tooth for a tooth.' Or to obey and imitate Jesus by stepping out of the realm of rights and into the realm of grace.

If we choose the second way, we relinquish our right to punish and, instead offer to the person or people who inflicted the pain undeserved, *agape* love—the love which seeks to find ways of helping rather than hurting the offender.

FOR PRAYER IN ACTION

Think of anyone against whom you have harboured a grudge or bitterness or hatred or with whom you have been angry. Ask God to give you the desire and the grace to let go of anything which would perpetuate the problem. Set these people free and demonstrate your own freedom in Christ by trying to find ways of blessing rather than cursing them.

Let go

We have seen the importance of forgiving those who have hurt or offended us but we have not defined what forgiveness really means.

To forgive means to 'let go' or to 'set free'. The Greek word is *aphesis*—a word Jesus uses at the grave of Lazarus.

Lazarus has been dead for four days so Martha protests when Jesus commands the by-standers to remove the grave-stone. 'But, Lord, by this time there is a bad odour . . .' Even so, the stone is rolled away whereupon Jesus turns his eyes to his Father, then gives the command: 'Lazarus, come out!' To everyone's astonishment, Lazarus appears, his hands and feet still wrapped in the strips of linen which served as grave clothes. 'Take off the grave clothes and let him go,' commands Jesus (John 11:39–44, NIV). And the word he uses here is *aphesis*—set him free.

So in the last section we simply took the first faltering steps towards forgiveness. Now we can complete the journey.

Having remembered the injury or insult and made the choice to step out of the realm of rights and into the realm of grace, next we must let go of any bitterness or hatred or resentment we have been bottling up inside us. If we fail to do this, we remain in bondage to the person who has hurt us. They are not yet free and neither are we.

I sometimes illustrate this by clinging to a chair with both hands. While the chair fills my hands, my movements are severely restricted and so is the chair's usefulness. When I let go, however, a miracle takes place. I am free. And so is the chair.

The same is true of forgiveness. When we let go of the negative feelings which have been poisoning our minds and hearts, God lances the abscess and cleanses us from all the pus which has collected inside us. We enjoy a whole new beginning and so does the person with whom we have been locked in conflict.

FOR PRAYER

Ask the Holy Spirit to show you if there is any particular person you are treating with the harshness Jesus warns against. Ask for the grace to repent—that is, to determine to live differently—to remember that love is kind.

Refuse to condemn others

When someone has hurt or offended you, don't take revenge but rather love them, pray for them and forgive them. These are the suggestions Jesus makes as he helps us to handle relationships creatively. To this catalogue of seemingly impossible requirements, he adds another: 'Do not judge . . .' (Matthew 7:1, NIV). Commenting on this command, William Barclay, the famous Scottish Bible commentator, observes: 'There is hardly any commandment of Jesus which is more consistently broken or neglected.'[1]

I fear he may be right. Families and fellowships, friendships and marriages fly apart because Christians seem to be unwilling or find it impossible to take this command seriously. If you doubt that claim, listen to yourself thinking about some of the people in your circle of friends and acquaintances. Or listen to the gossip which goes around the office or the neighbourhood or the church. Bring this under the torchlight of this verse as we try to tease out its implications.

By making this request, Jesus is not advocating the disuse of our critical faculties. These are gifts to be used, among other things, to distinguish between right and wrong and to receive discernment. No. Jesus is challenging us to continue to swim against the cultural tide by refusing to become fault-finders— the kind of people who seem to take sick delight in the perceived failures of others, who exalt themselves by running others down, who look at their own lives through rose-coloured spectacles while assuming a jaundiced view of the lives and attitudes and ministries of others.

This way of thinking is as pernicious as Aids. Turn your back on it, Jesus advocates. Refuse to pick holes in the ideas or lifestyle or attitudes of others. Refuse to mete out destructive criticism or sarcasm. Refuse to exaggerate their faults while patting yourself on the back as though you were perfect—or nearly so. Refuse to cast a slur on another's reputation. For such treatment of others is cruel. It crushes them, belittles them, stunts their growth and harms the fellowship. Replace it with kindness, gentleness, love and prayer.

An exercise

Building on Jesus' teaching, Paul once wrote:

Love is very patient and kind,
never jealous or envious,
never boastful or proud,
never haughty or selfish or rude.
Love does not . . . hold grudges and will hardly even notice when others do it wrong . . .
If you love someone you will be loyal to him no matter what the cost.
You will always believe in him . . . and always stand your ground in defending him.

1 CORINTHIANS 13:4–7 (LB)

1. William Barclay, *The Gospel of Matthew*, volume 1, The Saint Andrew Press, 1975, page 266

Ask God to give you that kind of love in increasing measure.

A more excellent way

I once had to have surgery very near my left eye. It helped me to realize how sensitive to touch that part of our body is. It also gave me an insight into the meaning of the parable Jesus told to illustrate the teaching we have been examining: 'Do not judge . . .':

'Why do you look at the speck of sawdust in your brother's eye and pay no attention to the plank in your own eye? How can you say to your brother, "Let me take the speck out of your eye," when all the time there is a plank in your own eye? You hypocrite, first take the plank out of your own eye, and then you will see clearly to remove the speck from your brother's eye.'
MATTHEW 7:3–5 (NIV)

If, while I was lying on the operating table, I had noticed that my surgeon had a plank poking out of his eye, I would have panicked. How could he possibly see clearly enough to perform a delicate operation on *my* face? That is precisely the reaction Jesus wanted to produce in his listeners when he asked his string of questions.

Put your own house in order, he seems to say. Until you do, you have no right to criticize or condemn anyone else. And even when you think your perspective is clear, you are still in no position to judge another. You do not know their full story: the temptations they face, the background which has helped to make them the people they are today, the hurts and deprivations they have suffered, the quirks of their psychological makeup, their innermost longings and motives.

So always err on the side of kindness. Only the faultless have earned the right to comment on the faults of others.

EPILOGUE: PRAY AS YOU CAN...

One of the wisest and most practical pieces of advice about prayer which has ever been given is this: 'Pray as you can, not as you can't.' I mentioned this at the beginning of this book and, quite deliberately, I want to end on the same note.

My present job takes me to a whole variety of countries. Very often I am in places where English is not spoken, yet, somehow, when I need to communicate with someone, we find a way—through gesticulation, drawing, pointing, miming—or through enlisting the services of an interpreter. The important thing at such times is not the method we use but the fact that, against all the odds, messages are given and received.

When we are learning the language of prayer, such flexibility and openness to experiment is vital. And even when we feel we are becoming more fluent in communicating with and listening to God, the willingness to try a whole variety of ways of praying continues to play an important part in our relationship with God. As Richard Foster puts it: 'One of the liberating experiences in my life came when I understood that prayer involved a learning process. I was set free to question, to experiment, even to fail, for I knew that I was learning.' He concludes, 'Real prayer is something we learn.'[1]

Others have described true prayer as a search and have drawn the conclusion that the reward of the search is to go on searching. My prayer is that, as we complete the task of praying through this book, God may give us the adventurous spirit which determines to go on learning, to go on searching

and to discover the deep-down joy which comes to those who
are found by God.

Richard Foster, *Prayer*,
Hodder and Stoughton

BIBLIOGRAPHY

I would encourage readers who would like to learn more about learning the language of prayer to read some or all of the following books:

Richard Foster, *Prayer*, Hodder and Stoughton, 1992

Richard Foster, *Celebration of Discipline*, Hodder and Stoughton, 1980

Sr Margaret Magdalene CSMV, *Jesus—Man of Prayer*, Hodder and Stoughton, 1987

Jim Borst MHM, *Coming to God*, Eagle, 1990

Joyce Huggett, *Listening to God*, Hodder and Stoughton, 1986

Joyce Huggett, *Finding God in the Fast Lane*, Eagle, 1993

Joyce Huggett, *Open to God*, Hodder and Stoughton, 1989

Joyce Huggett, *Prayer Journal*, HarperCollins

The following cassettes may also be helpful:

Joyce Huggett, *Teach Us to Pray*, Hodder and Stoughton

Joyce Huggett, *Teach Me to Pray*, Eagle